NOTES FROM THE TRAIL

ALEXANDRA KERRY

PRESIDENTIAL POLITICS
FROM THE INSIDE OUT

MODERN
TIMES

Modern Times is an imprint of Rodale Inc.

Rodale books may be purchased for business or promotional use or for special sales. For information, please write to: Special Markets Department, Rodale Inc., 733 Third Avenue, New York, NY 10017

Printed in the United States of America

Rodale Inc. makes every effort to use acid-free ⊗, recycled paper ♻.

Book design by Triboro

Photos courtesy of the author, with the exception of the following:

Pages vi-vii, 89, 90 *(top)*, 91 *(bottom)*, 96 *(bottom row, right)*, 106-107, 110-111 *(top)*, 139 *(top)*, 155 *(bottom)* © CJ Gunther Photography

Pages 78-79, 80-81, 88 *(bottom)*, 91 *(top)*, 92-93, 96 *(third row)*, 97 *(top row, right; third row, right)*, 102, 103, 112-113, 114, 116-117, 118 *(top)*, 119 *(bottom)*, 128 *(bottom)*, 130-131, 132 *(top row; third row, right)*, 133 *(top row, right; second row, right; third row, right; bottom row, left)*, 136-137, 138 *(bottom)*, 139 *(bottom)*, 140-141, 142, 143, 156-157 © Hector Mata/Getty Images

Pages iv-v, 82-83, 86-87, 96 *(top row, right)*, 108-109, 115, 134-135, 138 *(top)*, 144-145, 146, 147, 148-149, 150, 152-153, 158-159, 160-161, 162-163, 171 Dina Rudick © *The Boston Globe*

Pages 120-121 © David Hume Kennerly/Getty Images

Library of Congress Cataloging-in-Publication Data

Kerry, Alexandra
    Notes from the trail : a view on politics through the windshield / Alexandra Kerry.
       p.   cm.
    ISBN-13 978-1-60529-980-8 hardcover
    ISBN-10 1-60529-980-4 hardcover
    1. Presidents—United States—Election—2004. 2. Kerry John, date 3. Presidential candidates—United States—History—Pictorial works. 4. Political campaigns—United States—History—Pictorial works. 5. Elections—United States—History—Pictorial works. 6. United States—Politics and government—date I. Title.
E905.K47 2008
324.973—dc22   2008013910

Distributed to the trade by Macmillan

2   4   6   8   10   9   7   5   3   1   hardcover

To Julia Thorne
1944-2006

CONTENTS

PREFACE

The face may change, but the composition remains the same: the headshot in three-quarter profile, noble or triumphant, against a slightly blurred background of red, white, and blue bunting; a legible campaign sign, if you get lucky and have a smart advance person who knows how to compose real life for the camera's frame. The parade of photographs and video clips for television blend into a vast abstraction, and the blur of sounds and images can mean only one thing: campaign season.

In 2004, I joined my father, John Kerry, on the trail in his bid for the United States presidency. In 2008, I'm on the sidelines rather than at the center of the scrum. I pass newsstands on my walk to work in New York City, the candidates staring out from the covers of newspapers and magazines, and I am flooded with conflicting emotions: exhaustion, euphoria, weariness, anxiety, joy. To many passersby these figures clutching podiums are familiar to the point of invisibility; to me these images are windows into memories of everything that happened beyond the camera's frame.

My relationship with the journalists who covered the campaign was complicated. I often hid from the critical eye of their cameras and their omnipresent digital recorders, wary of the critique implicit in every captured moment. But I also grew to respect and understand their passion for their work, their love for the journey we were sharing. A journalist is supposed to present an unbiased portrait of an event, a view devoid of intimate emotions. This is impossible, of course. The framing of an image, by its very composition, represents a choice. The photographer chooses what to show and what to exclude. In studying film, I learned how different a given moment can seem depending on where you put the camera. The close-up of the lover's smiling face tells one story. The close-up of his hand shaking tells another. If we see only the first picture, we will think that all is right in his world; when the second is added, we know that his smile is hiding a much more nuanced emotion, and the story deepens.

Some might say that when it comes to campaigns, we have already seen far too many images of these manufactured moments. I believe there is another narrative, one that is deeper than the carefully edited and tidily packaged story news editors choose to tell.

I watched the journalists on our campaign as they watched us. I watched them jockeying to get to the front of the line to board yet another flight, sleeping in hotel hallways, peeking toward the front of the plane for a chance at that one shot their colleagues would not be able to get. There were other times they let their cameras follow where their gaze strayed, to what was instinctively interesting to their eye, even if not considered newsworthy to their editor waiting back in the newsroom.

We are saturated with visual imagery. Most of our perceptions are based on what we are told, on symbols constructed by the press corps and photographers chosen to reinforce the angle major media outlets want to illustrate. But really, very few people read news stories in their entirety; instead, they hear a sound bite or read the two-line caption accompanying a photograph. It is not a chronicle; it is a single blink timed with a single breath. Words have great cumulative power, but in the 21st century, a single image is much stronger. An image suggests the unvarnished truth. That is its power and its fiction.

Our news outlets feed us images that correspond to the symbols we have come to expect, but moments of nuance and complexity still exist. Perhaps in part because they resist being boiled down into black-and-white categories, these moments generally are not considered newsworthy, and they certainly don't resonate in a YouTube world. As I came to know some of the journalists covering my father's campaign, I realized that they were all capturing a tale that was more personal, perhaps even more revealing than the easily digestible one displayed on the nightly news.

I often had my own video camera pressed against the car window as we moved down highways cleared of other vehicles by the Secret Service officers who preceded us. Beyond our own reflections, it's hard to see much of the world through the window of a moving car. I had set out to make a film about the campaign. I recorded, logged, and labeled 300 hours of video footage, but I never cut the movie. When I sat down in the editing room in November, I had only just lived the campaign, and it quickly became clear I didn't yet have enough distance to tell the story. The images may one day make their way into a film. For now, some are in the pages of this book.

On this road trip, I considered myself lucky to have other eyes, other cameras that were able to stand still when I was moving and capture moments that otherwise might have been lost. Now that the dust has settled, now that the barrage fed to the public by the media no longer includes me or my family, I can see these photographers' outtakes for what they are: vital expressions of my own experience as well as theirs.

Along with the images we expected to see, they also snapped photos we didn't predict, shots of the small, normally forgotten details that accumulate during a campaign and reveal its rougher, truer character. Some of these images appear in this book alongside stills of the footage I shot myself, and they—I hope—provide a different perspective on the parade of political heads and a closer look at a process that is vital to our country.

Each successive presidential campaign is more costly and waged on a grander scale than the one before. The 2008 campaign has already shattered fund-raising records and marshaled larger volunteer forces than the campaigns that preceded it. Yet somehow we, as Americans, feel more and more distanced from the political processes that are the underpinnings of our democracy. I hope my anecdotes and images convey a little of what I learned: That the day-to-day experience on the ground of the presidential campaign is grueling and hard-fought because it truly matters, and that behind the poll numbers, there are people, full of humor and grace and dignity, and sometimes anger and fear.

In his novel *White Noise*, Don DeLillo writes about "the most photographed barn in America." People traveled from all over to photograph the barn simply because it was the most photographed barn in the country. Once they had seen the road signs for the barn, DeLillo writes, it became impossible to see the barn itself. "Being here is a kind of spiritual surrender. We see only what the others see. The thousands who were here in the past, those who will come in the future. We've agreed to be part of a collective perception. . . . They are taking pictures of taking pictures."

Campaigns are very similar to the barn. We have become numbed to the photographs and experiences we have been taught to see: candidates kissing babies, eating ribs, hunting, fishing, golfing, relaxing with their families. These images tell us nothing because they reinforce preconceived notions. My hope is that a few of the pictures collected here will surprise, reveal, provide a different perspective, and remind us that behind the image of the barn is a genuine structure, one erected by real individuals who designed it and hammered the planks to form a building that would withstand weather and provide shelter.

The same thing applies to our electoral process. Behind each of the well-worn images are real lives. If we imagine the scene beyond the camera's frame, we'll see the full panorama, the vibrant existence of people whose stories intersect, and through this process, have the power to change.

1

PRE-ELECTION

If there is such a thing as a typical child of politics, I am not it. I did not grow up in Washington, DC. I did not run for class president. I wasn't trotted out at dinner parties to display my prodigious command of current events. I was the kid who stared out the window during political science class, who heard the teacher's voice as white noise to my daydreams. It wasn't because I disliked school or education—I knew the material mattered, I enjoyed learning, and I was encouraged to push hard to excel. A passion for political science didn't run in the family. What was happening outside the classroom window made much more of an impression. I would watch the late-summer skies of Boston turn gray, followed by the sudden, snapping colors of fall foliage, then the blue and white landscape of winter, and finally the brown tips of the exposed branches slowly taking on a tinge of spring green. From somewhere a million miles away, sounding to my disinterested ears like the muffled trumpet squawk of Charlie Brown's teacher, came tales of what some guys in strange wigs had done years ago in Washington, DC. I was distracted, capturing images framed by the window, busy composing movies in my mind.

Years later, I would look through another window, this one in a bus, watching Iowa's quilt-square hills eventually give way to Illinois's factory towns and then to Wisconsin's dairy farms and finally to Michigan's cities, and think to myself that a presidential campaign can be a lot like political science class—not always able to hold my attention. Government represented someone else's interests, not my own.

When I was growing up, my father brought home politics like a baker brings home an extra loaf of bread. It was simply his job. He always included my younger sister, Vanessa and me in his work, more to enable him to spend time with us during the course of his busy day than because we had budding interest in politics. While campaigning for his first US Senate race in 1984, he invited us to the "office," which during the summer months before the election meant somebody's living room. From my child's-eye view, that meant floors carpeted with shag and tables filled with plates of cookies and other boxed treasures I wasn't to touch even though I badly wanted to. I played on those rugs with other children who made me feel at home in strange towns full of people I'd never met and would never see again. Traveling to and from these "offices" often meant enduring interminable car trips. Sensing our boredom, my father tried to convince us we were on "important nature drives" by noting the foliage we passed or, in winter, the bulky blue shadows that suggested what lay beneath the white blankets of snow. I followed the thread of the world through the windshield as I grew.

If the sights proved uninspiring, he entertained us with songs or recited one of his favorite poems, Rudyard Kipling's "Gunga Din." When he stopped singing and began to practice his speech, we knew we were near our destination. While I understood as well as a child can that my father's job was serious and that the stakes were always high, our trips to events felt lighthearted. Once we arrived, the spotlight of attention trained on my father in these living rooms offered an early glimpse of what was to come. The attention was rarely directed at me. I sensed it only peripherally, rarely glancing up from my busy games of make-believe. As a result, my memories recall a normal upbringing, out of the public eye. My mother lived in Boston; my father voted and lobbied in DC. Vanessa and I always resisted becoming that political archetype, the candidate's daughter, and after our parents' separation in 1982, our family did not look like a smiling Christmas card come to life.

Before then, politics entered our home through familiar rituals. I knew it was time for another political dinner when my mother's room was filled with the scent of Krizia perfume. Although I never thought of my glamorous, slightly rebellious expat mother as a political wife, she'd open all three of her closets, pinning back the doors like shutters on an old stable, and rifle through her clothes to ready herself for an evening of icy policy conversation. I'd sit among her high heels and pull on the hem of each dress as she tried it on. I welcomed those occasions because they gave Vanessa and me the chance to manipulate our babysitter into allowing us another half-hour of *Sanford and Son*, though we had to pay for the privilege by acting as guinea pigs for her college child-psychology course. We studied Rorschach inkblots to the filtered sounds of laughter and clinking dinnerware. I tried to decide whether to say I saw a ballerina in the dripping swirls or to reveal the truth—that I glimpsed a vampire's fanged face that made me shudder. I always went with the ballerina, worried that if I confessed to seeing the vampire I would be carted away to the college's psych lab to be hooked up to some sinister machine that looked like a vacuum cleaner.

When I was older, I'd come downstairs some mornings, my hair still wild from sleep, and encounter attractive young men loitering sheepishly in the doorway, waiting to drive my father to work. They looked unsettled in their dark suits, like a row of suburban commuters waiting on the platform for a late train or a row of pigeons balancing on a wire, ready to be startled from their perch. At first I thought it was because they were concerned that they were taking him away from his family, but later I understood they were anticipating an hour of white-knuckle driving as my father directed them through parking lots and across medians, seeking "shortcuts" just this side of the law.

The staffers became more familiar to me over the years. I came to know aides, campaign advisors, managers, chiefs of staff, consultants, and assistants so well that at times they felt like family, especially when I padded down to the kitchen for a late-night snack only to find them huddled there, having already picked clean the plate of leftovers that had been my target.

As a teenager, I decided with the earnest solemnity of adolescence that I wanted to keep my relationship with my father, which I cherished, separate from my relationship with politics, which I regarded with cautious remove. I began slipping away from photographers when they entered our home, and ironically, while I was running away from cameras, I found my interest in filmmaking. Vanessa and I grew up with different orientations but with a common quality that was important to both our parents: independence. At least they said it was important when it suited them, but they were frustrated when it translated into stubbornness or a well-reasoned explanation for having missed curfew. With so many personalities in the house to contend with, my sister and I developed strong wills, which had both positive and negative implications. Vanessa followed her fascination with creatures with fur and fangs into medicine, becoming a physician. She journeyed to places like Ghana to learn about and fight the AIDS epidemic. I journeyed to Los Angeles and New York to study acting and film. Vanessa found herself in operating rooms, and I stationed myself behind a camera. We traded stories about our wildly divergent experiences. I told her of movie premieres and losing light on set while she complained about rural roads in Rwanda that are impassable after floods. In our own ways, we were both entering foreign lands.

While politics initially drove me to zealously avoid the camera, I ended up studying film and making it my profession. I had thought art and politics could not be farther apart, yet my life somehow merged the two in the most personal of ways, and I ended up filming the campaign. Maybe this shouldn't have been surprising—politics has a way of fusing fact and fiction. Because over the past 50 years so much of the national conversation has taken place on television, there seemed to me no better way to understand a campaign than with a collage of moving images. Maybe bringing my video camera on the campaign trail was in some way an effort to protect myself—after all, you don't go to a shootout at high noon unarmed—but I was also interested in documenting my experience, as well as those of others. It was my way of using the language I felt most comfortable with to enter a dialogue with the part of my life I had kept at arm's length and had an uneasy relationship with at best. So there I was on one side of the camera as the director, while most people wanted me on the other side as the subject.

When I was younger, I was as comfortable with my own company as I was organizing a secret protest or party in the playground. I was as happy spending an afternoon by myself out in a field, following the progress of a group of ants struggling to bring home their booty of a crumb, as I was being at the center of some lively birthday party. I was the one who would run off during a game of hide-and-seek, forget that I was supposed to be found, and wander back only after everyone had begun to get worried. I had a tendency to get lost in my reveries, and sometimes being pulled back to reality was jarring.

When my father officially announced his presidential candidacy, my instinct was to avoid the process and focus instead on filmmaking, but another part of me knew I could not escape. Americans have come to expect prospective First Families to audition for the role, and with few exceptions we line up and perform like actors on a stage, potential protagonists of a play with numberless authors. The absence of one of the key characters does not go unnoticed, and it is often taken as a sign of disapproval. Although I had many reservations about stepping unrehearsed into my role, I was intrigued by the process.

In the spring of 2002, during our Christmas vacation, my father had been diagnosed with prostate cancer. An operation followed, and then months of discreet recuperation. Although it was clear he had decided to run for president, he waited for a clean bill of health before moving headlong into his campaign commitment. Told he was cancer free after the operation in early 2003, his run for the presidency was a celebration of sorts for us; a real battle had already been won.

By then, I knew my life would change; I would have to put my career on hold and subsume my life in a campaign that would be hard-fought and long. It wouldn't matter that I would carry a camera as a talisman from my world into his. I was expected to play a large role, and I knew that my relationship with my father—always kept separate from his job—would shift. I expected that new friends, media people, campaign staff, opponents, consultants, and opposition researchers would enter our lives, pry into our world, pick apart our flaws, question our morals, promote our image, and spin our words for even the slightest political advantage. I was aware of how people—and their families—aspiring to high office are treated by the media. I had a certain degree of natural or assimilated political instinct and intuitively understood the workings of the machine's components: the staffing, fund-raising, propagandizing, message crafting, and voter reaching. Yet, despite all this, I was a neophyte. In previous local campaigns, we would pile into a Crown Victoria and travel within one state. This time the vehicles would have to be larger and faster than a leased old car, considering the ground we needed to cover.

There was no official call, no embossed invitation formally asking me to "join the campaign." No one asked anything of me directly because no one needed to—in a political family, everyone is prepared to contribute with creativity and committment when the time comes. In spite of the sense of duty, in spite of the seeming inevitability of it all, I felt at first that ultimately the choice was mine: I could sit passively on the sidelines and smile for the cameras when prompted, or I could allow myself to be seduced by expectations and invest in the campaign.

I was wrong. The choice was made for me, not in one decisive moment, but gradually, over days and weeks during which I connected the landscapes beyond the windows that had fed my imagination to the political processes that had been background noise for so long. Politics not only came to life for me in a series of places and the people who lived there, it embraced me so wholly that at times it threatened to consume me.

I was lucky that in those first days all that was required of me was to try to decide which sneakers to pack and how to get from my apartment to the airport. From the early primary campaigning in winter 2003, when the prospects for the nascent Kerry campaign's survival were not auspicious, to the comeback primary victories in early 2004, to Election Day, November 2, when my father lost to incumbent President George W. Bush, my life was spent on the road. I set out on what I thought would be a scenic afternoon ferry trip. It turned into the equivalent of a transoceanic voyage where necessity transformed me, without my noticing it, from passenger into crew member; I did whatever I could to keep the ship on course. Everyday life was a distant memory; the natural rhythms of my daily rituals were disrupted. Even when I did take a day off, there was no escaping the campaign. By then I always had one eye trained on the headlines, unable to ignore the images in newspapers and on televisions that at any moment might take a particular form suggesting a positive trend or a devastating reversal. I saw my experiences interpreted in the news like reflections distorted in a water's current.

You know how this story ends. There is no suspense in that. With this book I do not intend to explain the election or the American political system; both would require a bird's-eye view I didn't have. Rather, I hope to share some personal stories about what happened along the way, to describe what it felt like to play a part in a uniquely American process that most of us see only from the outside. I had thought I would be able to straddle the gap, to step in with one foot while keeping the other out to steady myself. I had planned to position myself, with my camera, as a voyeur of the campaign rather than a full participant.

In retrospect, it was naïve of me to think that I could watch the campaign from the eye of a lens. Like any fiercely contested battle, this one required every able body. Though I later grew to appreciate the work of the campaign, it always found other, more intrusive ways to expose my life and thrust what had been private into the public glare. I, like my father, first learned from investigative reporters at the *Boston Globe* that I had a Jewish great-grandmother and that my great-grandfather had committed suicide in the men's bathroom of a Boston hotel room. Potentially painful family revelations were played out for the world as reporters waited for a response. I saw my father's character distorted in attack ads. His wife, Teresa, my stepmother, was dragged into the fray as all political wives are. The details of my identity, my heritage, and my family would all become fair game.

An actor friend of mine who had more than 30 years of political involvement told me campaigning would be like traveling 1,000 miles per hour in a comfortable chair. It was more like being attached to an EKG monitor on speed. I spent grueling weeks in Iowa and New Hampshire, and then, as if all at once, there were 33 additional states. The laws of time and space seemed to warp according to levels of adrenaline, fatigue, and endorphins fed by sugar and caffeine.

And then, when I finally felt like I understood my role and had come at last not only to love what we were doing, but to be convinced of its great importance, the campaign was over.

If, in the big picture, the election was polarizing, with people choosing between "the high road and the low road," up close the masses of united voters dissembled into individuals with unique agendas. Banners that read "Save Our Water" competed with union signs advertising fire brigades and teamster brotherhoods. Children were painted red, white, and blue. Men and women screamed, their voices hoarse reminding me of fans at rock shows I'd been to, although they weren't all dressed in requisite jeans and hippie skirts. Inconsolable people tried in vain to convey the breadth and magnitude of their fears in a few brief moments along the rope lines, and others offered treasures: lucky coins, homemade dolls, their grandmother's sweet bread. I felt daily the tensions inherent in democracy, with large voting blocs composed of distinct people with complex life stories who might all vote in the same way in order to say something different.

At the beginning, to look out into the crowd from the side of the stage and see singular faces was at once uplifting and disarming. I had never seen so many people: Midwestern farmers with soil still on their blue jeans; construction workers who walked, fearless, on steel I beams above us; young mothers who brought their children to witness history; retirees with folding lawn chairs in case their legs gave out.

I remember the freckled cheeks and dangling earrings of the woman who handed me a Coke, wrapped in a damp paper napkin, when I came offstage in Alabama. I associate the taste of the brownie given to me in Fort Worth with the chapped hands of the woman who had baked them and transported them in stacks of Tupperware. I wondered about their lives, what had motivated them to bake at dawn or leave their house that day, what series of decisions had led up to our paths crossing for an instant.

Today, these small gestures combine in my mind to form a composite of generosity, an aliveness in the so many people I met, but they also feel like lost, hazy moments. The significance of those personal interactions was never fully realized because I was too busy remembering them while they were happening to truly live the experience. Aware of how fleeting each moment was and how hard it would be to recapture, I was already nostalgic as events played out. Memory folded over on itself, leaving me constantly and instantly wistful.

Politics is conducted on such an epic scale in America. Partially this is by necessity. The country has grown from its origins as a narrow union hugging the Atlantic coast into a nation stretching across the continent. So many more voters with so many more divergent concerns still pull the levers of a system designed in a very different age. The system expands, at times almost to the breaking point, to include them all. There are consequences to this evolution. A general election has become a juggernaut so massive that it's easy for people to feel invisible and to decide that it's not worth a single voice because, in the grand scheme of things, one vote just won't matter.

I didn't vote in the 1996 election. Many of my friends didn't either. Despite my upbringing and all of the exhortations to the contrary, we felt no compulsion to take part in something that seemed so disconnected from our experiences. We had our heads down, busy struggling in our first jobs after college, trying to figure out what shape our own lives would take. We were a far cry from the young people my father recalled with admiration from his own early days in politics: the idealistic activists who sacrificed their spring break to take buses down south to organize black voters, or who wholeheartedly joined the "peanut butter and jelly brigade" of Senator Eugene McCarthy's presidential campaign, with its platform to end the war in Vietnam. Whatever change had taken place over the course of a generation had left apathy in its wake. As far as my friends and I were concerned, it was pointless to choose sides. There was very little difference between politicians.

It was hard to imagine how we had gone from the liberating political activism of the 1960s, when protesting was the norm and families lived and breathed current events around the dinner table, to the drone of sound bites on CNN and the common advice that it was best never to discuss politics in polite company. Apathy has a curious negative strength of its own.

In college, I thought the volunteers who accosted me about one political candidate or another as I made my way across the quad had drunk a bit too much of the Kool-Aid—I thought they were more lost than I was as I headed off to the next music festival to dance in my batik-print skirt. Their loud yelling and fluttering flyers seemed like an overreaction, or at the very least a gesture so lacking in the self-consciousness I felt at the time that it was alien. I was so busy learning and describing the outlines of my own emerging identity that the larger world and things as abstract as politics seemed beside the point.

I eventually learned that an individual doesn't necessarily lose anything by becoming part of something larger than themselves; as a matter of fact, coming together around a shared passion satisfies a very primitive and essential human instinct whether found in religion, family, or a film set. The scenes that stay with me from the campaign trail are the chaotic, almost apocalyptic visions of the rallies. For me the election was about passion—it was what we saw, what we felt, what we heard. Whether politics had always been this way and I had been an outsider unable to see the powerful feelings it evoked, or whether there was something truly different about 2004 in particular, I can't say.

Certainly there were reasons that the 2004 election had particular importance. The first attack on American soil since Pearl Harbor had made invulnerable America suddenly vulnerable. Launching the biggest military campaign since Vietnam had opened old wounds, making them new again.

But, as always, on the individual scale, the issues were nuanced and complicated, threaded through with memory and emotion. At home in Los Angeles, reading the newspaper in a coffee shop, I realized that the conversation of the older married couple next to me wasn't the familiar political banter or the dry academic back-and-forth of smug public policy think-tank fellows. The couple was engaged in an argument charged with profound personal resonance. Between increasingly vicious bites of a sandwich, the husband railed against the war in Iraq. As he crumpled up his napkin, he reminded his wife of Vietnam.

"Of course I remember," she said, exasperated.

"Well, why does it seem like nobody else does?" he asked. Filling his wife's judgmental silence, he assured her, "I am no bleeding-heart liberal."

"I know that," she snapped. There was no need for him to tell her. He had voted for Schwarzenegger, she needled him. She pursed her lips and, without looking up from her coffee, began talking about the phone call she had received from their daughter in New York City that morning. Her daughter couldn't stop thinking about September 11, she said. She was having a hard time leaving the kids at day care because she was worried she'd never see them again. Then the woman looked her husband in the eye. "Why does our daughter have to be afraid?"

He stared back at her, and then looked at his plate without an answer.

I, too, was perplexed by the question even as I embarked on a journey that sought in part to address it.

9

2

IOWA

Months before the Iowa caucuses, when candidates' stories were still buried deep in the middle pages of newspapers, my father was fighting what looked like a losing battle. He was running a distant third in the informal polls.

I went to join what most people were calling a dead-on-arrival campaign. My father was an afterthought, portrayed as an also-ran by the national media as Howard Dean's upstart grassroots campaign gathered what seemed to many to be unstoppable momentum.

Before my flight from Los Angeles touched down at Quad City International Airport, I knew little about the Hawkeye State beyond the classically bicoastal, insular images of Grant Wood paintings of small-town life I had seen in museums and history books. On this sullen day, there were no hay bales in sight, no county fair chock-full of the deep-fried corn dogs I had heard so much about. Just empty fields with a five o'clock shadow of gray. The day reminded me of waiting at the outdoor subway station when I was growing up in New England, shivering, shifting from foot to foot to stay warm, overhearing old men, their hands stuffed into worn coat pockets or cupped around Dunkin' Donuts coffee mugs, muttering, "It's too cold to snow."

And so it was in Iowa. Too cold to snow. Maybe the real Iowa had more in common with my home state of Massachusetts than the Iowa I had come to expect from the hastily assembled made-for-television movies that aired each holiday season. Certainly it had more in common with Massachusetts than Los Angeles ever would. Places I had imagined as foreign were so similar to the ones I already knew.

A campaign volunteer about my age drove me across the Mississippi, straight to the Davenport Marriott to meet my father for a round of barnstorming. Awkwardly shoe-horned into several parking spaces was a red, white, and blue bus, the so-called Real Deal Express the campaign had leased for this final stretch of months before the caucus vote. It was shrink-wrapped in logos and stained with road salt. I thought about how bizarre this bus must look to the men who stood outside the coffee shops and the con-struction workers who looked at us as we drove by. Here we were in November 2003, a year before America would go to the polls, 90 days before even a fraction's fraction of Iowans would cast their ballots in their precincts' caucuses, and slinking up to traffic lights was a campaign bus, as if it were election eve. No one could have been blamed for asking "John Kerry's running for president of what?" as the bus lumbered past, leaving behind a puff of exhaust in lieu of an answer.

But to that fraction's fraction of Iowans who did participate, who lived and breathed this process, this preliminary salvo of the presidential campaign represented the home-stretch.

The statewide Iowa caucus has been a sacred political ritual for more than 30 years. The caucus as we know it today represents reformers' reaction to the disturbing images of the 1968 Democratic National Convention in Chicago, when students and antiwar activists—supporters of Robert Kennedy and Eugene McCarthy's insurgent campaigns—were silenced by the old-line party bosses who called the shots and decided upon the nominee in those notorious cigar-smoke-filled "back rooms" of politics. Protests in the streets and confrontations at the convention center were hardly the images a self-proclaimed "party of the people" could tolerate for long, and so a national commission was created to figure out how to give the party to its activist base—to return power to the grass roots. Antiwar activists devised a plan to open up the nominating system so that the results reflected the will of the people. The commission also dictated that Iowa should move its caucus to earlier in the year so that there was ample time between the precinct caucuses and the caucuses at the district, county, and state levels. In ret-rospect, it made sense that Iowa went first as it was the birthplace of many historical populist movements.

This process, in which people meet in small groups to talk over the candidates' qualities and make their choice for president, didn't garner very much national atten-tion until Jimmy Carter's campaign. In 1975, with the nation reeling with disgust from Watergate and fatigued by the legacy of Vietnam, which had tested citizens' faith in government and their stomach for Washington, it was the peanut farmer, Naval Acad-emy graduate, and one-term Georgia governor who saw the potential of the Iowa caucus to upset the establishment. Governor Carter was not afraid of the repeated questions—"Jimmy who?"—or the mockery of the journalists with marquee bylines, if they drew attention to his nascent campaign in the most invisible of invisible primary seasons. The little-known governor ate dinner with Iowans—one by one. He even slept in their homes. With no motorcades and few staffers, street by street, neighborhood by neighborhood, he built a volunteer army. Carter spent more than 100 days in Iowa before the caucus. A playbook of his campaign could be called *While Washington Slept*. The establishment pols raised money with glittering fund-raisers held at the big hotels in Washington, DC. They signed up members of Congress to lend their impressive résumés to unwieldy steering committees.

But Carter knocked on doors in Cedar Rapids, Dubuque, and Davenport. The experts dismissed him as an amusing upstart. He introduced himself: "I'm Jimmy Carter and I'm running for president!"

In the first of many caucus night surprises to come, Carter received the largest percentage of voters in Iowa, creating the momentum that led him into the general election and finally to the presidency.

In the decades since, the Iowa caucus—followed by New Hampshire's primary—has become a fixture of the presidential nominating process. In a way, it has succeeded in doing what the 1968 reform committee desired, helping to diffuse the party's power and put the selection of the nominee back in the hands of the people, even if they are a choice group who happen to live in only one state. Like a gambler, almost any candidate with a dollar and a dream—or, even better, stamina and a few good ideas—can become an overnight sensation if he or she plays the cards right in Iowa. Political junkies refer to Dick Gephardt's "zero to hero" 54-point climb in the polls and Iowa caucus win in 1988, to the more recent cautionary legend known as the "Dean Scream" in 2004, and to Barack Obama's unexpected win in 2008.

Along the way, the political machinations surrounding the Iowa caucus became more sophisticated and intricate. Sometime around 1980, when Massachusetts senator Ted Kennedy ran an insurgent campaign challenging President Carter, Iowa became a magnet for green operatives eager to make a name for themselves. In 1980, young Democratic activists Steve Murphy, Ed Reilly, Joe Trippi, Jill Alper, Steve McMahon, Michael Whouley, and a host of others left college, bound for Iowa to set up shop for the Kennedy and Carter campaigns. By 2004, they were the campaign managers, pollsters, and senior advisors for the Dean, Kerry, Gephardt, and John Edwards campaigns that topped the Iowa caucuses. Iowa became the place where national political operatives had to get their tickets punched.

For the national press corps and the punditocracy, as well as the Democratic establishment, the lesson learned from the Carter upset was "Fool me once, shame on you; fool me twice, shame on me." After 1976, the press began looking more deeply into the implications of winning in Iowa. They weighed the necessity of following up with a win in the New Hampshire primary. They tried to develop ways to separate diamonds in the rough from one-hit wonders. They attempted to gauge the advantage a politician from the Midwest might have on his home turf. They wondered whether a candidate who opposed ethanol subsidies—federal money allocated for producing Iowa's homegrown alternative energy source—was committing political suicide or exhibiting political courage.

In 1988, Massachusetts governor Michael Dukakis proudly spun his strong third-place finish, declaring he had "won the bronze medal." He used this bounce to springboard to friendlier turf in New Hampshire. In 1992, the Iowa caucus was judged almost moot when home-state favorite son Senator Tom Harkin jumped into the presidential race, setting up New Hampshire to turn a certain Arkansas governor into the Comeback Kid.

I'll leave it to professionals to determine the historical significance of caucuses, whether campaigns can truly be won or lost in states that make up a mere fraction of the total population. But, as we saw in the primary season of 2008 and as I know from experience, surprises happen in Iowa.

Our bus was not just a means of transportation, it was literally the engine of the cause. The candidate and his skeleton crew of early advisors shuttled from stop to stop, hoping each one would not be the last. It was shortly before Halloween and the reporters looked as though they felt some cruel trick had been played on them, ensconcing them on a horrible bus to nowhere.

The Real Deal Express was not an idea or an image for those reporters; it was a drafty hulk of aluminum that they lived inside. Empty cold medicine packets, drained coffee cups, discarded Diet Coke cans, and endless wrappers of rapidly devoured candy bars littered the floor. Wet leaves lay buried like sediment under tracked-in road slush. I felt as if I'd stepped into the Old Testament scene in which Jonah hangs on for dear life inside the belly of the whale.

The bus was a mobile medical unit. Everyone aboard was sick. These were not polite coughs, but deep and phlegmy hacks. All of it emanated from the reporters berthed in the bus's stern and seemed to mist forward, spreading the human equivalent of a kennel cough. It felt as if this campaign swing might be better recorded in a petri dish than in a notebook.

The reality of life onboard wiped away any last illusion I had of the legendary characters from Timothy Crouse's book about the reporters covering the 1972 presidential election, *The Boys on the Bus.* I found an empty seat between an advance man and a surly reporter who sighed as he changed positions in the midst of some dream that was undoubtedly set in a warmer, more welcoming climate. I moved a stack of wilted McDonald's salads, sat down, and contemplated how I might be able to get the smell of ranch dressing out of my coat.

The first thing you learn about small-state retail politics is that you will pay almost any price and bear almost any burden to "break through." In the movie industry, a breakthrough is a role that alters the course of a career, but in politics it's more like breaking through the ice into bracingly cold water—exhilarating for some, but chilling for others. It means—just for an instant, almost as if on a dare—breaking through the noise, the clutter, the conventional wisdom.

The staff huddled in the middle of the bus, hashing out the strategy for Iowa, many of them having gambled their reputations on its success. There were many times during these early days of the campaign, days that many secretly felt might be among its last, that the staff energized themselves, putting aside their fears and resolving to accept the night's outcome and move forward with unchecked enthusiasm. I watched advisors and staffers work with what seemed to be the feverish energy of the doomed and witnessed, in the midst of utter exhaustion, the surreal spirit that can sweep through a campaign. I noted the way the staff ignored the reporters huddled at the back of the bus. Not only were they trying to do something many observers were saying was impossible, they were doing it while under the microscope of the press corps. I was reminded of nature documentary footage in which a herd of ibex grazes peacefully at the watering hole, either unaware or unafraid of the pack of lions lazing just a few yards away.

Growing up, I learned quickly to avoid reporters. I had nothing against them personally. In fact, in college I became the editor of the weekly paper. I looked up to progressive essayists and practitioners of New Journalism. Having seen journalists loiter in our hallways, I was always curious about what the other side was about. I fantasized about Joan Didion pecking piercing words on a typewriter at some beachfront desk.

But a childhood and adolescence spent cautiously skirting the edges of photo ops and interviews made me distrustful of the political activity that seemed to be an imposition on my life. Because I couldn't ultimately avoid these press moments, I learned what it meant to be caught on camera, to endure people observing with pen and notepad the awkward indignities of adolescence, and most of all to be of interest to the media primarily because you're a reflection of someone else.

Speaking my mind when I was 12 and less comfortable with my thoughts was hard enough at the dinner table, particularly when my father challenged us to be clear about our opinions and points of view even when they contradicted his own. "Too many 'likes,'" he would whisper through a mouthful of shepherd's pie. When I announced that I was becoming a vegetarian, my father asked me my reasons. After I described the horrific treatment of animals at slaughterhouses and the environmental degradation caused by the waste runoff from cattle ranches, he pointed to my leather shoes. "What about those?" he asked. "Well, these are like . . ." I protested. Even when I knew he had a point, I had to defend my position and provide proof for my stance. It was his parenting style.

My parents influenced my personal opinions and beliefs, but I developed my own worldview. The public persona I took on for the Iowa campaign was an extension of my father's. With the stakes so high and the reporters in such close proximity, I faced what seemed to me to be an impossible situation: being an appropriate spokesperson for the campaign without losing myself in the process.

I had entered a tiny, confined space with the media—it was like being in a submarine that gave no sign of surfacing anytime soon and was filled with my lifelong adversaries, who were now dependent on cough syrup, grouchy, and listless. But these were not the older, grayer, lumbering journalistic specimens I was familiar with in Boston. These were young recruits fresh off the J-school conveyor belt, still reeking of college newsprint. They bet their analytical skills and their sheer physical endurance on the possibility that the candidate they had been assigned to follow might somehow emerge as the Democratic nominee. Part of it seemed to come down to the luck of the draw—the reporter assigned to the Bush campaign in 2000 secured an eventual White House beat, while the reporter assigned to Gary Bauer's flight of evangelical fancy ended up in the tuba section of the journalism parade. With their career prospects so clearly intertwined with the ups and downs of the subject to whom they were assigned, manifesting Stockholm syndrome was a strong possibility. It was understandable that they might be unable to resist the temptation to identify with a particular side—it would be like trying to write about the prospects of the horse you were riding in the Kentucky Derby. Still, green and idealistic, many of them had decided to try to be professional dispassionate observers, remaining apart from the action while unmistakably part of it. I studied their faces for signs of weakening resolve, and in the moments they weren't otherwise occupied, they studied me right back: the older daughter, freshly arrived from Los Angeles, with no campaign experience to speak of. At first, before my role became clearer and I found my footing, we kept to an uneasy truce.

Within a week, Iowa became less foreign. By virtue of the repetitive rhythm of our days, I ceased to be a stranger. I became a part of the routine. When the bus pulled up to our first stop of the day, a construction site, we disembarked. In the mist of a wet morning, cameras lifted into position, and I stood back, looking through the lens of my own handheld. My father was doing in Iowa what I'd grown up watching him do countless times in Massachusetts: wrapping his long arm around someone's shoulders, leaning in with his good ear to hear better. I watched the press slide into place on the floor in front of the bleachers at our first event. On their knees, lined up in rows, they looked like kindergartners waiting to be read a story. They needled out words, strung sentences together in their notebooks, wrote banal stories about what the candidate wore when. In the early, grueling days of a primary, the small details are the important ones to the press and, as a result, to the candidate.

The press crafted narratives from the ground up, falling back on the types of physical description used by novelists to differentiate characters. The goal was to fill column inches, to find some kind of human hook to engage an editor or a reader before the outlines of the larger struggle had become clear. They did not yet have the rolling ball of the national conversation to participate in or pile onto.

At the mercy of their news organizations, they had the difficult task of meeting deadlines from the back of a bus, sending in stories remotely at 3 a.m. I watched them type under the spotlights above their seats, struggling to hit the proper keys through wool gloves, embroidering the delicate details of what they called "color."

Standing on the fringes of their conversations, I felt like an intruder. I realized that many of their questions had predetermined answers. They wanted me to comment on why my father wasn't wearing a hard hat at the construction site, where he had gotten his new-looking, scuff-free work boots, how the workers gathered around him at the site had been selected, whether or not there was any substance behind what seemed to be just another staged photo op.

Dissatisfied with my answers, they resorted to another old reporting standby: numbers. The number of minutes spent at the construction site multiplied by the number of workers and divided by the number of hours on the road apparently could determine whether the 24-hour workday was political folly or political genius.

As they rattled off calculations, I had the vague feeling of panic I used to get when I opened the math portion of any standardized test. I began to understand the stakes involved in a seemingly small event like a potluck dinner or a town meeting. It had a sense of theater, the excitement of a live performance, and I realized that our audience was not only the people attending the event, but also the group of reporters who stood ready to disseminate their reviews of our little play to the wider world. I developed a greater understanding of their power, of that thin line between our side and theirs, between contrivance and truth, the point at which our emotions became their sound bites.

A hunting trip outside Des Moines turned into a Talmudic discussion among the press corps about whether a candidate who favors limited gun control was having it both ways by shooting geese. The Iowa campaign manager wanted to introduce my father—a hunter since he was a kid—to a fellow hunter who happened to be one of Polk County's most prominent Democratic activists through the common language of tracking birds across the autumn sky. It was not just about hunting and what kind of message that sent, it was about personal politics, about two people sharing an afternoon, the Iowa chief argued to the unconvinced press corps.

"Then why are we here?" asked the suspicious *New York Times* reporter.

"The problem is, you're everywhere," deadpanned the Iowan.

The reporters seemed as interested in the ideas being debated as in what was going on underneath the hood. For every campaign stop, they wanted to know who the target audience was and how we intended to reach it. The attitude seemed to rest on dual presumptions: Everything is a stunt, and everything is political. And then came the dissection and analysis. "What did the stunt mean?" Had it in the end been positive, negative, convincing, or all of the above?

The press was evaluating the candidate like prospectors assaying a rock they'd dredged out of a river. There was a scientific attempt to determine the elemental composition of my father's accent. To some it seemed he had retained his New England a's and r's; to others it seemed he had deliberately lost them. When we found a crowd of 40 campaign loyalists who'd come from a sign-making party, braving the late hour to see him, we had gained support in their eyes. But when we dropped by an all-night bowling alley at midnight, it was perceived as a failure—only seven voters sat by the alleys waiting for a handshake and the possibility of bowling a strike. We had only been off the bus for 35 minutes before the press corps returned to the pregnant sartorial issue of the moment: whether the candidate's bowling shoes were the same as everyone else's, or if the advance staff had somehow reserved a nicer pair. I wasn't yet seasoned, merely excited by the parking lot asphalt under my feet and the chance to bowl a spare in the middle of the night. I snuck around the back of the bus to call a boyfriend who was far away. I couldn't explain the scene or my exhaustion to him and just watched my breath in the cold air, wishing it was smoke from a cigarette.

The press and staff were opposing forces who traveled together but had different goals, the my-side-or-yours mentality personified. Then, suddenly, there was an about-face: a 4 a.m. stop at the Hy-Vee to buy warm donuts. The bags were passed around, filling the bus with the sweet smell of freshly fried dough; all of our fingers were covered with powdered sugar, and I saw the partnership and shared goals between the groups.

On the campaign trail, sugar ameliorates tension and fuels adrenaline. We scrambled after sweets in the supermarket as if we were five-year-olds descending on a just-broken piñata at a birthday party. At 5 a.m. on that same morning, we visited county maintenance workers who were heading out to salt, sand, and clear the roads. At 6 a.m, we were beside the *Des Moines Register*'s printing presses as the morning edition rolled off the belts, witnessing the news cycle in production and the small company who executed it. I am sure a courtship was also occurring between the *Register* and my father so that he could win their endorsement, which only helped fuel the national press' impression that this was one more seemingly textbook moment on the road. Later, this frisson between local and national media outlets would become a major collision.

We had all come together over donuts, and not two hours later, we closed ranks again. Stories filed by the national reporters concluded that the visit to the printing presses was a stunt that had fallen flat. They darkly suggested that perhaps it was a metaphor for the entire campaign: being at the wrong place at the wrong time, making time for the photo op instead of meeting with voters. The local Iowa reporters who'd been on the trail with us knew Iowa more intimately and presented a different take. They had seen my father bowling, shaking hands, visiting diners, eating pie, traversing construction sites. And in spite of his unscuffed boots, they had concluded that perhaps there was something to him as a candidate.

This difference of opinion seemed only to annoy the national reporters as they came down from their sugar highs and shuttled off to various small airports to travel home for Thanksgiving: places like New York, Boston, Washington, Atlanta, and Los Angeles—anywhere but Iowa. I didn't tell my father about the criticism I had overheard in the back of the bus, and his advisors also protected him from it. Many in the press had proclaimed him a "dead man walking."

One commentator had floated the idea, a few others had seized on it, and soon it became the commonly understood analysis. New to the trail, I couldn't piece together whether these critical portrayals were unsporting attacks on a candidate or accepted reportage. Their repeated questioning of my father's "everyday Joe" bona fides, his suspiciously fancy shoes—which were supplied like others from behind the counter—seemed so foreign to the election's issues that it often felt like they were playing out some kind of collective personal grudge. In hindsight, I realize I was bearing witness to a ritual. The writers were exercising their critical faculties to try to get at the truth underlying what sometimes must have felt to them like frustratingly orchestrated tableaus with little substance.

After a stay in Los Angeles, I arrived back in Iowa days before the caucus and found Des Moines had been transformed into a real-life Brigadoon, a bustling hub of all things political that burst onto the national political scene every four years before disappearing again. The unrelentingly gray landscape had turned into a contrast of white snowy fields and bright blue skies. No county fairs, but everywhere a carnival atmosphere.

The grainy black-and-white images now had the instant gratification of Polaroid color. The difference between the level of energy in that lone rattling bus and its new incarnation with every seat filled by additional staffers and reporters was not subtle. Something had changed, not just in Iowa, but also in the campaign.

The political staffers deposited for months at a time in Cedar Rapids, Iowa—the self-proclaimed city of five seasons, with the fifth season being "the time to enjoy the other four seasons"—knew that there is karaoke at the bar at the Crowne Plaza Hotel. Assigned to various towns across the state, they knew the map coordinates of every Tastee Freez. The Stop and Shops, Safeways, and Food Lions they'd grown up with were nowhere to be found, so they learned to look out for Hy-Vees. Instead of 7-Elevens, there were Kum and Gos, providing fodder for many crude jokes. They knew to time their morning drives to the office. At exactly the right moment, they rolled down their windows and breathed in the sweet, chalky smells of the Quaker Oats factory. Some even claimed to be so versed in that experience—half automotive, half culinary—that they could hold court on which flavors of instant oatmeal were being prepared inside the factory walls that day. The Waterloo, Iowa, field operative knew the story of the city's World War II "Fighting Sullivans"—inspiration for Steven Spielberg's *Saving Private Ryan*—and the locations of memorials dedicated to those brave sailor brothers, and perhaps had even met a Sullivan or two at a diner.

Long lines of bigfoot national reporters jawboned with Deaniacs in orange hats as they jostled for lattes at Des Moines's one and only Starbucks before heading out for long days of grassroots precinct walking, phone banking, and muckraking. Field directors for each campaign, who called to mind 19th-century carnival barkers, moved vast hordes of volunteer manpower and recent college graduates to counties targeted according to some magical numerical formula they called "caucus weight." They pored over maps and charts and polling data, looking for the silver bullet that would propel their candidate ahead of the nearest rival. I walked down Locust Street in Des Moines, passing formerly vacant storefront windows now covered with campaign signs: "Dean for America." A huge banner spanning two buildings boldly proclaimed, "I See Dean People." Repeated in Warholian fashion, "Gephardt for President" signs were taped one next to another, filling the floor-to-ceiling showroom window of a one-time used-car dealership.

I was driven to my father's makeshift headquarters along campaign row and stepped inside the great melting pot of a campaign as it neared the finish line. The Bostonians

I had seen and heard in my house growing up were present for the final push, adding to the cacophony of accents in the small room's complex soundscape. The easy-talking Midwestern warmth of the Iowa activists, the flat, cutting Dorchester vowels of our homegrown operatives, the giggles of the high school volunteers, the occasional crying of toddlers dragged into the headquarters by mothers or fathers who either wanted them to be a tiny part of history or couldn't find sitters on short notice. The textures of sounds filled the space: the staccato rustlings of checklists being reviewed, the rise and fall of jokes and banter, the muffle of whispers, the private strategy confabs punctuated by the occasional loud yell—someone had received good or bad news.

Like a college athlete grown into middle age who predicts rain when his football knee starts acting up, my father always said that around election time, he could feel a different electricity. I hadn't known what he meant until now. For me, election time had signaled the end of the back-to-school season, when our backpacks didn't seem new anymore.

Now, as I saw voters jamming the phone lines, newspeople swarming Des Moines, college kids giving up their holiday vacations to flock to Iowa, I understood. The election was the finish line, and every gesture mattered.

Middle-aged national newsmen in long, expensive overcoats got back in touch with their inner cub reporter, with the spirit that had first compelled them to care enough about politics to endure years of bumpy bus rides and bad food to cover campaigns; young campaign staffers waged snowball fights with their counterparts from rival camps, enjoying the fleeting moments of relief from the rough-and-tumble of a hard-fought process; volunteers brought in tray after tray of homemade meals for workers who hadn't seen home, let alone home cooking, in months. Under a cloud of cigarette smoke, aspiring Masters of the Progressive Universe congregated at Chequers, the bar at the Hotel Fort Des Moines, at the end of long days, swapping stories, spinning reporters, looking to the left and to the right for the captain they'd either be hiring or asking for a job, depending upon what the Fates had in store for their candidate on caucus day. Something that had seemed so alien, so impossible to penetrate, something I had dreaded and reluctantly decided to become a part of only a few weeks ago, had become my world. It was as if we'd collectively begun by hitting a flat tennis ball against the side of the garage and then suddenly found ourselves at Wimbledon.

The Real Deal Express had not turned from a pumpkin into a coach, but it too was different—it had gone from sparsely populated to densely packed. In the very back, the reporters had commandeered a curtained-off area and christened it the Champagne Lounge. In a version of shuttle diplomacy, my father faithfully retired with them each night to down a longneck beer or a hot concoction cooked up to soothe his raw vocal cords.

Vanessa had been campaigning in Iowa longer than I had—I was mostly back in Los Angeles attending classes, acting, working on a film. As a result, Vanessa had become well versed on the stump, right down to her applause lines. She could effortlessly memorize binders full of facts and figures that supported my father's positions on every issue. For a while we were to be teamed up as a sister act, a one-two punch to warm up the crowds before my father's events. I cringed at the thought of the performance, it seemed treacly and trite. We started at house parties of 20 or 30 potential voters and moved to 300- and 400-voter events at community college theaters and high school gymnasiums. I nervously watched my sister mount the political stage with calm and poise.

Hot lights shone from above. We walked to the center of the stage in a high school theater set up in the round. Past the glare of the spotlights trained on us sat a restless audience, their energy heightened by the possibility that the man who might be the next Democratic nominee for president would soon arrive.

Then I heard the words performers no doubt have dreaded since before Shakespeare's day: "He's running about an hour late. We need you to stall for time."

"What do you mean by 'stall'?" I asked.

"Get up there, talk to the audience, and stall for an hour."

An hour. He might as well have said a week. It seemed like a giant blank canvas stretching before us, one I had no idea how to fill. The feeling of being in a school play came rushing back to me. What if I forget my lines? The problem, however, was worse than that because I had no lines. We were supposed to make up the play on the spot.

Vanessa and I fell back on what we knew best—a sister act comedy routine we'd perfected on family vacations over the years, most of which had been designed to embarrass our father when he was behind the wheel of the family car or trying to cook dinner as a single father. We told these same stories of our father getting up early on Sunday mornings, making us pancakes in the shapes of animals, his fierce competitive streak rearing up as we demanded more challenging shapes. A mouse. A llama. An octopus. Various species of monkeys. There were the misshapen images my father would pretend were truly exotic breeds—extinct in some cases—from way before our time. To us, stalling for time on that stage, the stories seemed ridiculous. I couldn't believe this was all we could come up with. It was like a bad date.

The audience nodded. Maybe they liked home-cooked meals. Or maybe I was tuning in to something I'd forgotten about politics. Television commercials and candidate forums of nine or ten Democrats debating a few dimes' difference in competing proposals to raise the minimum wage doesn't draw much of a clear distinction. My father's Real Deal Express, John Edwards's One America Caravan, and Howard Dean's Prescription for Change Tour had a way of canceling each other out.

The Kerry health care plan might or might not have been better than the Dean health care proposal. But here was a family member relating the conversations she'd had with her father at one or two in the morning as she endured her first weeks as an intern at a hospital, learning to live with the limits of what a doctor can expect to achieve. She spoke about how he told her that the nature of the job was to try to do her best, even if she measured herself at only 60 percent, to see each patient as an individual, to remember that she was there to serve all of them, however difficult that might be. This seemed to resonate with audiences who wanted to vote not for the issues, but for the kind of man they would like to have in office, the kind of man who could understand them. I learned the lesson firsthand that politics is personal. Even anecdotally getting to know a candidate cuts through the blur of attack and counterattack. The retail politics of the Iowa campaign is far more intricate than house parties in neighbors' living rooms; it is the process by which Iowans get to be the first in the country to test whether they could live with the man in the White House—and in their living rooms—for the next four years. It seemed to resonate with them; if they could meet his child and understand how he raised her, they might feel better, worse, or at least differently about how he might decide to send their own sons and daughters into harm's way.

More than I had realized, voters desperately wanted to know not just what you thought, but how you felt and who you were. In Iowa, I discovered there is a purity to the process. Say what you will about the citizens of one little state being so important to the national political machine, but these caucus-goers took their responsibility very seriously. Once I understood that they had come to see us so they could try to make an informed decision, my stage fright subsided.

My struggle to balance protecting my father with being true to myself disappeared. If I just told the truth about the kind of person I knew him to be, people would respond. There's a raw and compelling innocence in the act of asking whether you can trust someone not just with your vote on a wintry caucus night, but with the power of the presidency—the power to react to a Pearl Harbor or September 11—that justified the listening and the litany of questions.

Maybe they wouldn't find the answer in our homespun tales of my father struggling with a stove top or pretending we weren't lost on long walks in the woods, but it couldn't be found in talking points either. Here in the middle of America, Iowans were telling us what we should have known instinctively—what I should have known as a filmmaker: Cut through artifice to capture the real spirit of a subject first and foremost. It is about character.

Sometimes I felt as if the reporters treated the candidates like films to be reviewed. My friend confided that one late night after the reporters thought my father had fallen asleep, he had heard a Boston-accented scribe speculate on his cell phone about how soon Kerry would drop out so he could take his long-awaited vacation. But there were also isolated incidents of unexpected behavior, such as a reporter confiding in another newbie that the process had suddenly become "magical."

Winter had already set in, and the checkerboards of farmland were frozen over with a milky glaze of snow. We toured one small town after the next, separated by long stretches of road. The farms were defined by their dirt-road edges, each field ordered and smoothed as if a fine-tooth comb had grazed it. As time compressed, space seemed to expand. No matter how much ground we covered in the last 48 hours, it would never feel like enough.

The hours on the bus were grueling, and each stop was a part of the countdown to the reckoning hour. I spent the moments between towns pressed against the windows, watching the sky. The highway seemed endless; snow turned brown with the sand dumped by the snowplows in the early hours of the morning.

As the caucuses neared, the strategies that had been put in place long before seemed to be paying dividends. Michael Whouley, the campaign's Iowa strategist, had implemented a local network with deep roots in order to come out on top in a process that had so much to do with personal conversations. My father started giving what was dubbed the "Two Roads" speech, which was designed to clearly distinguish him from his competitors.

The serendipitous arrival of my father's Swift boat crewmen was actually a surprise. Del Sandusky seemed to appear out of nowhere, eager to share his recollections about how my father had saved lives in Vietnam. And then, just as miraculously, a retired policeman from Oregon, Jim Rassmann, came upon Douglas Brinkley's book about my father's Vietnam experience, while wandering a bookstore in January 2004. Rassmann, a Special Forces soldier, had fallen into the water during a firefight on the Bay Hap River, and my father had swung the boat around to get him. When Rassmann read the book, he recognized his own story and called the campaign. The next day, he and my father reunited in Iowa. For us, it was an incredibly moving moment and also a slightly surreal one, taking place as it did in front of the cameras.

In those final days before the Iowa caucus, I began to feel something shifting, as if plates were moving beneath the ground, the possibility that we could actually win. Yet, none of the media, except the *Des Moines Register*, who had projected my father to take Iowa, stated the same. I know journalists who have confided that they knew something was about to happen during those last days. But not all of their papers printed it.

After decades of journalists studying the caucuses and vowing never again to be surprised by the dark-horse victory of another Jimmy Carter, years of academics perfecting "political science," months of representatives of nine hopeful candidates methodically calling Iowa home, hundreds of carefully orchestrated bus trips, motorcycle rides, motor home excursions, state and county fair visits, backyard barbecues, buttons, flyers, pamphlets, and door hangers—all the momentum built up to this least scientific of caucus-day moments: the candidate on his hands and knees, searching the floor of his hotel room at the Hotel Fort Des Moines for his lucky four-leaf clover.

My father was scheduled to attend a Catholic mass before the caucuses, but he would not leave without his pockets full of the lucky charms he had gathered over a lifetime and that seemed to have multiplied in Iowa. It was no longer just the dog tags secured in a pocket of his briefcase and the St. Christopher medal tucked beneath his white undershirt. Now it was also a lucky tie, a lucky pocketknife, three lucky coins handed to him when luck had seemed at best elusive and at worst a cruel joke, a lucky hat, a prayer book Max Cleland had given him, and the latest addition to his collection, a four-leaf clover sealed in cellophane, a gift from an Iowa farmer just a day before.

He was not alone in resorting to ritual when reason offered no comfort. Staffers who had lived and breathed this campaign from the very beginning, who'd prided themselves on methodically turning a fledgling operation into a humming machine, had fallen under the deepest spell of superstition and sentimentality. It had seemed haphazard at the beginning—kids just out of college bunking on the couches of a lone supporter. Now, the campaign was running with the precision of an efficient machine. Still, as my father's poll numbers rose in the final week, his earliest Iowa ally insisted on eating the same lunch at the same restaurant at the same time every day, convinced there was a psychic connection between this daily decision to eat roasted chicken with grilled vegetables at the Beggars Buffet and the decisions of 15,000 Iowans who would be reached at home by a pollster that evening. Setti Warren, his trip director, always went to mindless movies on election day, as if to acknowledge that the outcome was now in the hands of a higher power and that, besides watching *There's Something About Mary*, there was nothing more he could do. My dad's friend from Dorchester, Massachusetts, wore the same black baseball cap with the US Marine Corps insignia buried behind a brim that was perfectly bent.

I still have not figured out why those in politics have such a deep need to believe in luck, in karma, in a connectedness between seemingly unconnected events, objects, and memories, while at the same time they pride themselves on economy, efficiency, and logic. There is simply no way to explain why a man who had spent months in meetings building a health care plan that harnessed market forces and anticipated the returns of introducing technology in the health care market seemed now to believe that his political future—the future of his ideas, the fate of his carefully vetted policy proposals, everything—might be helped by a four-leaf clover hermetically sealed in cellophane.

Caucus day in Iowa was no different than any other election day, with the last-minute barnstorming of the usual places—fraternity houses, nursing homes, labor halls, VFW posts, rally sites. I looked for hints of energy among the press corps; we had picked up a few more people along the way, which seemed like a good sign. I visited a caucus site for my last chance to prod, plead, and persuade and discovered that time was accelerating. In a huge high school auditorium crammed with people, all the thousands of house parties came together, with young activists bartering T-shirts and buttons for a last-second consideration of their candidate, a cacophony of voices.

Campaigns start small with long conversations, but they climax amid the pushing and shoving crowd. With little sense of whether you'll affect anyone, you try to project a smile that you hope says something to as many voters as possible.

I remember entering a screening room in the basement of a building at the University of Iowa. A man named Eddy stood listlessly against the moss-colored wall. He said he was "taking in the vibe" in order to decide whom he would vote for. Energetic undergrads ran around with last-minute appeals for their candidate. A man I had met the night before at a firefighters' famous chili feed flashed me a gray-toothed grin and said he knew "what corner he would be standing in" just as somebody passed him three more candidates' pins. Two veteran caucus-goers embraced like aging baseball players. Every four years, it seemed, they were on different sides of a campaign, but tradition and a beer bridged any gap between them.

When it came time to caucus, we were ushered out into the snowy air and the door was closed behind us. In the cold silence, I was tempted to stand on a trashcan and peek through the window at this secret society with its own rites and rituals. Like Catholic cardinals during a papal conclave, Iowans make this final judgment in secret. All we could do now was wait for the telltale puff of white smoke.

The process in Iowa begins in the spring when Iowans open their homes to candidates seeking support and accumulating staff members. It grows in the summer with hopefuls' appearances at the county and state fairs, and finally explodes in the fall when the entire political universe descends on the state. It brings more political hacks than you can shake a campaign sign at, with camera crews from around the world knocking over precious family mementos and violating the sanctity of the living room meeting. There is something fitting about the intimacy with which the process ends, how it comes down to an exchange of opinions behind closed doors.

While they caucused, we looked at each other cautiously relieved by the fact that we could no longer claim control over something we knew we had little influence on and dodged eye contact awkward with expectation. It felt uncomfortably like waiting outside the principal's door in elementary school to find out which excuse would prevail in explaining why you had skipped class. I couldn't keep my legs still.

As a kid, I remember staying home from school with the chicken pox, watching 1950s sitcom reruns, fascinated by an episode of *I Love Lucy* in which Ricky Ricardo—dressed in typically absurd fashion as a cannibal—rushes from a performance at his nightclub to join Fred and Ethel at the maternity ward waiting room, filled with dozens of expectant fathers, smoking cigarettes nervously, celebratory cigars at the ready.

On this night, I felt as if we were all inside the tiny black-and-white television screen, anxiously anticipating the results as if they were a sitcom star's baby. My uncles and other men in business suits crowded us, so many of them familiar to me from similar scenes that had been staged in our kitchen earlier in my father's career. Only now the group that assembled to play the waiting game had grown exponentially since I was a little girl. Max Cleland was there in a black and red flannel shirt and blue jeans, holding court about veterans' turnout. Crewmates of my father's from Vietnam, men I had previously known only as the subjects of a few grainy photos on the top floor of my father's house in Boston, were there captured at a distance by the camera. Women moved around the edges of the room like fluttering birds, putting their requisite parkas on and taking them off in nervous syncopation as they went outside and just as quickly came back in along with the cold air that clung to them. Staffers hurried back and forth, folding and unfolding and passing around notes on tiny ripped pieces of paper. It combined to create the sense of an elaborate, old-fashioned quadrille, with dancers weaving between each other and shifting directions seemingly unexpectedly, but all in accordance with some larger pattern.

A local news channel called it for us first.

Phones rang. Congratulatory calls were placed and received. A staffer ran out to get ice from the hall machine for the cheap champagne.

And there wasn't a minute to savor it. I tracked the images with my camera but had begun to feel pulled by living the experience and watching it behind a lens. I had brought along my friend Tanaz, a documentarian, and passed the camera back and forth schizophrenically as I traded roles of observer and participant. Before I had time to process what was happening, the experience rolled into a photo-opportunity version of itself. One minute we were watching the television, the next minute we were being watched watching the television.

"Okay, we'll be doing a quick 30-second spray of the family—just the family—here on the couches, maybe one quick question, then they're out," said an aide I'd never seen before. And before I had time to conjure the gruesome visual of what a "spray" of a family on the couch might look like, the door opened—the media entered—herded like cattle threatening to stampede—flashbulbs wild and bright—video cameras now Beta, not the tiny handheld digital video cams the press had had earlier in the campaign. The press corps—a pool, they called it—swarmed.

The reporters yelled in unison:

"Senator, howdoesitfeelwhataboutnewhampshirehaveyoutalkedtogovernadeanto-nighthowdoyouthinkthishappenedthiscomefrombehind?"

3

NEW HAMPSHIRE

The winter morning regulars at the diner in Manchester, New Hampshire, idly sopped up their eggs with triangles of toast and went over the week's gossip, unaware of the three buses unloading outside, discharging the rumpled mass of 50 press people who set out across the green lawn between the parking lot and restaurant. The crowd that jostled through the doors disrupted the breakfast ritual. Forgotten hotcakes swelled with syrup. Sticky-faced children craned their necks to see what all the fuss was about as the press pushed between the chairs. A man with ruddy skin and stubbly cheeks, dressed in a flannel shirt, winced as a large microphone hit him in the back of the head.

We navigated the restaurant at the head of the pack as if we were pieces on a chessboard with no squares—all purpose and no order. Within this intimate space people would be won over by a handshake, the glint in an eye, the solid answer to a question. We made our way table by table, covering ground measured in inches, one possible vote at a time, veering off course only to avoid the occasional Bush-Cheney pin spotted in our path. We stopped to win a point, turn crisis into calm, or politely comment "good pie" when a piece was offered by an eager proprietor who couldn't have known how many slices we'd already sampled that day, how many there were still left to eat. I leaned against a glass display rack that spun around like the prize rooms on *The Price Is Right* to show off the frothy height of the lemon meringue pie and the gooey layers of chocolate cake, desserts as incongruous to breakfast as we were to the quiet morning.

Just as quickly as the stampede had entered and filled every square of free linoleum, one of the herding advance team gave the word and we departed. The press filed out of the café, pushing against each other as if they couldn't wait to get off of an uncomfortable amusement park ride. Somewhere in South Dakota, a family was watching this scene in New Hampshire unfold on their TV screen. It was unclear who we were targeting with those visits: the people in the café or the people watching at home. I can't say whether we won any votes between the forkfuls of hash browns that morning.

By the time I began to process the experience, I was already on the lawn of the next diner, the doors swinging open to reveal more hands to shake, more faces welcoming us or blocking our path. It would have been easy to miss the cue and fall by the wayside or get trampled underfoot in the rush to keep up the pace. I focused on the numbers that gave our movements a semblance of order. We had four more establishments to visit before lunch. Two bowling alleys to see that afternoon. Three bars to drop by that evening. And in the following days, eight rallies to attend.

The drive from Manchester to Concord is not terribly long—about 30 minutes—and it should be a relatively pleasant ride past a few quaint towns tucked amidst the forested roadsides. But on one particular trip between these cities, days before the New Hampshire primary, the short journey seemed to stretch to an interminable length. I sat in the back seat of a small black Honda, wedged between the campaign's New Hampshire press coordinator and a fresh-faced young woman who had just graduated from college and been assigned to cover the New Hampshire primary for a big-city paper with a limited national circulation. The two made small talk across my lap.

"The last time I was in a car doing an interview was for my college newspaper with Charles Ogletree," she said as we hit a bump and her pen jostled on her pad.

The countdown began in my head: 5, 4, 3, 2, 1 . . .

"So," the press coordinator asked with a sad sigh of inevitability, "you went to Harvard?"

"Well, I don't like to drop the H-bomb, you know," she said, starting with a bray then trailing off.

You just did, I thought as we exited for a rally at a Manchester high school. She went to join the gathering group of reporters and I took my seat on a folding chair at the back of the stage. Speaking to the ever-larger crowds drawn to hear his message by his success in Iowa, my dad had learned how to simplify his message, especially when he talked about one of the central issues, the war in Iraq. He spoke about how his combat experience in Vietnam would influence the choices he would make as commander in chief. When he mentioned the friends he had lost, you could have heard a pin drop.

I was reminded of the junior reporter when her story appeared in the paper the following morning. No reference was made to anything issue-based that anyone had discussed. It did, however, nail the crimson tint of the candidate's tie. To me it seemed that instead of finding the story within the complexity of the issues, she had fallen back on mundane details that reinforced preconceived ideas about the candidate and were entirely beside the point, but easier to get her pen around.

At some point opponents and then the Bush campaign had spun a story of cultural separation between my father and average Americans. "He even looks French," they claimed. His habit of speaking in long, complete sentences further proved his suspicious intellectual predilections.

It was this sort of coverage—this need for caricaturing, for drawing stark and artificial lines between the candidates by painting one as a regular guy who liked to have fun and the other as an out-of-touch, elitist, flip-flopping liberal—that got in the way of ideas and policies that really mattered to people's lives. In truth, both candidates were products of the same boarding school-and-Ivy League educations. My father was not the flip-flopper the opposition painted him as, and President Bush was more substantial than his caricatures made him out to be. Not only did the campaigns of both candidates suffer from the overly simplistic portraits, the issues at the heart of the campaign suffered, sidelined as they were by these ad hominem attacks.

My time in New Hampshire was shortened by a visit to my mother, who had traded in her capes and heels for cardigans and corduroys as she endured another round of chemotherapy. My visits east had been split between time with my father on the campaign and visits to my mother on an oncology unit. As the primaries began, my mother waged her own battle with a type of urinary tract cancer. Close to two months before the primaries began, sometime in October, she had been diagnosed with transitional cell carcinoma. I was in Los Angeles when my cousin Beth arrived unannounced in the editing room to tell me the news. The rest of my family, my mother, sister, and stepfather, were in Boston already where she was undergoing her first of several operations. Because I was so far away, they had sent a family member to tell me in person. She had been diagnosed in Bozeman, Montana, where she was living, but had spent several days in Boston confirming the test results. Within 24 hours she was in the operating room undergoing surgery to remove the tumor.

Since the campaign had begun, I had a strange vision of somebody coming to the editing room to tell me something had happened to my father. I had imagined walking numbly down the steps of the building to a car waiting to drive me away to the next scene. I had never imagined it would be my mother. Beth and I walked up to the top of Griffith Park and sat in silence, swatting away bees. The operation took eight hours. I had already learned, from the previous months on the campaign, how to stay myself through the liminal period of waiting for information, for results. But the shock had quieted me, and I had no idea how to respond, so I clung to the facts. The tumor had grown in the lower part of the left ureter. She would have to undergo chemotherapy for several months before having a left nephrectomy, an operation to remove her left kidney. But the human body could easily function with one, and we were told that the prognosis was "good."

Following several doctors' suggestions, she had moved from her home in Montana to a rented house in the Boston neighborhood I had grown up in to begin treatment at Massachusetts General Hospital. The green fluorescence of the hospital rooms where she sat with an IV in her arm created the same unease in me as the holding rooms on the campaign trail did Vanessa and I struggled to share the strange journeys being undertaken by each of our parents in worlds that could not have been more different but also informed each other and echoed with uncanny parallels. While we elaborated on our father's public message, we created a wall around our mother to hide an illness she begged us to keep secret. We alternated between peeking from behind the curtains of the bus to see phalanxes of people waiting for change, and sliding similar curtains across our mother's bedroom windows to give her privacy and allow her to rest.

Whichever world we stepped into, we hoped abstractly to win against forces larger than us, fighting for outcomes we didn't have definitions for. We spent a great deal of time waiting.

I remember many holding locations—the places where we would loiter until a scheduled appearance—that had a down-the-rabbit-hole strangeness. If a rally was at a school gymnasium, then the holding room might be a teacher's lounge, and although we all congregated there around the boxes of cookies provided by a local volunteer, I couldn't shake the residual feeling from childhood that by being in the teacher's lounge I was somehow transgressing. Schools were common places for campaign events not only for the large meeting spaces but for the convenient parking—often free after school hours. Crossing the state in the latest incarnation of the bus, I paced the free-throw lines of many polished wooden gymnasium floors and made more than one phone call from a principal's office. I leaned against the heavy velvet curtains of stage after stage, never tiring of the youthful thrill of impending performance evoked by the cat's-paw of that fabric against my skin.

As I shuffled along salmon and beige and yellow squares of linoleum at one school, I tried to push from my mind the tiles' similarity to those of the hospital corridors I had just paced briskly when visiting my mother post-chemotherapy. I moved through the hallways telling myself to concentrate on the rows of lockers, breathing the astringent smells of industrial cleaners, the bracing ammonia in the lungs, feeling the ache of the reassuring innocence of childhood that the nicked and dented gray metal conjured, wishing fleetingly I could wrap myself in that battered armor of adolescence.

Windows lined the corridor in between classrooms filled with bulletin boards decorated with construction paper cutouts, visual aids for reports on animals from around the world. Penguins were a universally popular choice. In the classroom where the advisors gathered, pasta-art family portraits rendered in dried macaroni, fusilli, and rigatoni shed bits and pieces to the floor as the Elmer's glue cracked. The group seemed to grow by the minute, as this or that bright mind was deemed indispensable to getting over the next hump, to making the most of the next push. They took their seats with the same straight-backed poise one might have at an executive conference table, adjusting themselves politely in 1-foot-tall plastic chairs at desks bearing the abstract swirls of finger painting.

Bob Shrum, the veteran campaign strategist, pulled his chair back to make room for his 60-year-old girth and adjusted effortlessly to his new grade school status. If it looked to me like they had all somehow been held back not 1 year but 50, they were completely unfazed and acutely focused on the job at hand, which had nothing to do with learning not to fight over toys or how to count to 10, no matter what the carefully lettered posters surrounding them might suggest. This most serious business, the behind-the-scenes of a bid for a job many argued was among the most important on the planet, occurred in a room with mats piled in the corner for nap time, with the latest poll numbers being passed around like graham crackers.

Downstairs in the basement, another tableau was unfolding. My father had not slept during the previous three days of campaigning, with the stretches of travel too brief to allow for any real rest. He had walked the same echoing hallways I had, in the same midmorning light combined with flickering fluorescence, but he had an air of late-night determination about him. He walked with purpose, as though he were looking for his hotel room and couldn't quite remember which number it was. Flanked by advisors who briefed him on the move about the latest refinements being made to positions on health care and the environment, he made a beeline for an empty science classroom. Skeletons hung from the high ceilings, the periodic table marched in timeless squares across laminated posters, faded formulas haunted the chalkboards like ghosts.

Unlike the rooms upstairs, which were lit by the vibrating light emanating from grated plastic squares on the ceiling, this room had a calming darkness. My father laid down on one of the black Formica-topped experiment tables. Eyes closed, hands clasped across his chest, an American flag positioned behind his head—for once, not engineered that way—he looked as though he was being given last rites. But it was only five minutes of sleep before 24 more hours of journey.

On the day of the primary, the campaign team split up in order to cover as many of the firehouses and commerce buildings serving as polling locations as possible. The idea was to have some kind of contact, however limited, with as many voters as we could. It was the first time I had been sent out into the field on the fly to ask voters if they had any last-minute queries. Although later I would grow more comfortable interacting one-on-one with voters and even lead long, multistate trips supported by a core group of staffers, at this point I felt exposed, separated from the group on the bus. I tried to push my feelings of futility out of my mind. Vanessa and I had been sent out together, and if we could manage to visit six polling places for a half hour each and speak with anywhere between 5 and 20 voters per polling place, then we could reach a grand total of maybe 75 voters, if we were lucky.

It was important to keep our spirits up, no matter how circumstances might bring on anxiety. We visited one out-of-the-way polling place tucked along an icy, snowbanked river. Sharp gusts of wind blew in off the water and through the diamonds of the chain-link fence that surrounded the building. Reading anything into our passing interactions with constituents who wanted to get in out of the cold wouldn't be useful and was unlikely to yield optimism.

We stamped our feet to keep the circulation going and leaned into arriving voters, trying to strike a balance between being cheerfully aggressive and respectfully distant. It takes a certain personality to walk that line and not feel in some way that you're being untrue. This was not my forte. But just as I managed to put my cynicism behind me, warm up to the task, and find the right tone of friendly banter, we received a phone call reporting that we were needed to fill out the Kerry contingent at a polling location across town that had somehow become the site of a spontaneous media event.

A volunteer drove us in our rental car as we fielded more and more urgent calls, asking for our updated ETA. After getting lost—a seemingly daily occurrence, especially in those early days before travel details were turned over to the precision of technology—we finally pulled up in front of yet another elementary school that had been turned over to election officials for the day.

Groups of Dean, Edwards, Kucinich, and Kerry supporters had gathered in the circular driveway with signs, pins, hats—whatever could be used to announce their affiliation. It was the convention writ small, with groups huddled together on their hard-won turf, taking over snowdrifts and corners of parking lots, chanting, waving signs, trying to attract the local press with their competing colorful displays of plumage. The reporters darted between the groups confused, their feathers less colorful, their movements coy as they tried to stay focused on the story but were distracted as this group sent up an elaborate chant and that one launched into some kind of choreographed number, waving their signs in coquettish circles like showgirls.

We spent the final voting hours of the New Hampshire primary driving down Main Street in a town whose name is lost to me now. Billboards loomed above no-name coffee shops and bars; the gigantic proportions of the ads' slogans made the town seem larger than it was. A white sign announcing in large black letters "God lives here" was immediately followed by one bearing an image of a woman in a transparent nightgown reclining as she chatted on the phone, her glossy lips parted in a delighted smile, along with her phone number, should one feel the need to talk. As is so often the case, sin was easier to get a hold of than God, who, although local, didn't provide a number.

My sister and I and a few friends who had joined us for this leg of the campaign were giddy with fatigue, which, although good for bouts of hysterical mirth, did not always help me think rationally. I was hypothesizing aloud, as though my plans and expectations could actually form a political narrative. I asked our driver what would happen next, seeking any bit of information, no matter how arbitrary. It was a time when people had few answers. Later, they would have more, although that wouldn't mean the opinions were more accurate.

4

SUPER TUESDAY

After the steadily building climb of Iowa and the culmination of New Hampshire, the campaign exploded into a free-for-all, with state primaries falling like dominoes over a series of weeks. The slow evolution of the American political process didn't take geography into account; if it had, states so far from each other wouldn't hold their primaries on the same day, forcing campaigns to undertake backbreaking travel schedules. We crossed the country using every viable and available means of transportation: planes, buses, trains, and RVs. If someone had put me on a donkey and slapped it to send me up a mountain, I wouldn't have blinked.

But just as much as it was an exhausting marathon, with many days on which all I could do was wake up in the morning and tell myself just to get through one more day on five hours of sleep, the process was also energizing, in no small part because of the people I met. Faces that blurred like confetti now fell into focus.

There were the voters battling serious illnesses, for whom getting out of bed and coming to a political rally was an act of courage and stamina in itself. They pushed their wheelchairs forward to the guardrail for a chance to reach out to someone who might be able to help them address the suffering that had brought them there. Others came not for themselves but for a larger cause. A woman stood trembling at a town hall meeting about stem cell research. Her body wracked by advanced Parkinson's disease, she fought to speak. When she did, her message was hardly defeatist. "It's too late for me," she said. "But goddamn it, it can still be won for others if we stop messing around and get on with it."

These were the people for whom the election was a means for connecting with someone or something that might be able to help them accomplish what they saw as their life's
mission. Some were systematic, with a calm dedication to a premapped plan of action.
Others were gripped so fiercely by their cause that they bordered on unbalanced. They
came in droves, with a sense of urgency rarely encountered in everyday life. Family members pushed photographs of a mother lost to heart disease into an aide's hands. Sometimes the requests were direct and urgent: Help an uncle struggling with prostate cancer,
which the family felt was related to Agent Orange exposure in Vietnam.

They didn't hate George Bush. They pushed forward to the front of the queue because
the government—nameless, faceless, neither Democratic nor Republican—kept sending
them form letters instead of helping them understand why something terrible was happening to someone they loved. They had exhausted all the channels, already spent too
many hours on hold. They didn't want the name of their congressperson; they wanted us
to hear them as individuals and to act. But there was always the next person to meet, the
breakneck schedule to keep.

The sound of swarms of people stayed with me; competing cadences, whispers, and
rhythms. The endless humming of testimonials repeated like rosaries. A 30- or 60-second
snippet of a personal story could be both unnerving and comforting, and often was
completely at odds with the next one: the mother in a "Support the Troops" T-shirt who
reached out and pulled me close to beg me to support her son by supporting the war—*They
need the country to know we're with them!*—and then the gray-haired father at the next
rally who felt the only way to support his son, also a soldier, was by bringing him home.

The Real Deal Express had given way to a 727 jumbo jet adorned with decals just like
the bus. Reporters decorated the cabin with personal mementos the way one would a
college dorm room or a military barracks. The World's Largest Thermometer in Baker,
California, or Whiplash the Cowboy Monkey at a rodeo in Iowa—were represented in post-
cards, snapshots, and cut-out headlines and articles collaged together that stretched all
the way to the back of the plane where the photographers kept each other company, odd-
ly separated from their pencil-wielding friends. The youngest reporters taped up pictures
of themselves barhopping along the Atlantic City boardwalk when the campaign had relished a day off there; the 35-and-older crowd posted pictures of their wives, husbands,
intendeds, or toddlers at home. The veterans of numerous presidential campaigns didn't
have the time or patience for these rituals. The cabins above their seats were pristine except for the ink smudges left by their fingerprints as they reached for laptops.

My father's quarters at the front of the plane were cordoned off from the staff section
in the middle by a thick polyester curtain. At the rear of the plane, the press's section had
more class levels than the Titanic. Photographers, camera crews, and junior reporters
representing lesser-known publications were all relegated to the back like second-class
citizens. Seating was fiercely negotiated, based on who had the widest circulation and
how the hierarchy had been established in years past. Aisle seats were at a premium because they allowed a clear view of the curtain to the staff's part of the cabin.

When someone was forced to give up his or her seat according to some obscure point of order, it was further proof of how people are constantly aligning themselves with different factions. From wars to family reunions, individuals guard their space or identity, looking for their place in the order of the universe. It stood to reason that those who cover elections would be compelled by the same impulses. I learned to think of the line between the staff cabin and the press cabin as a kind of demilitarized zone; in stepping over it, I left the ease of being with staffers my age for the always-on-the-record, everything's-fair-game land of journalism.

One day—an hour even—I'd be playing cards or having a backslapping conversation with the young reporters who were drinking beers around the bar at the back of the plane, and the next, they'd be asking me for a response to fresh news from the ground—Bush said what about Kerry today? Before I had time to formulate a response, the laptop computers sang to life, their keyboards rattling beneath the pounding of fingers of reporters under the stress of always being an hour away from deadline.

Older newsmen moved with the steady bulk of years of accumulated wisdom, weariness, and experience. They sank into their seats with the sighs of the ages. Some of them seemed to look at the world through ancient eyes, seeing not only the elections of the past 20 years but those stretching back even further into time. I wouldn't have been surprised to hear an anecdote about Lincoln, or a brittle invective about how everything had changed since women won the vote. One minute they might be dismissive, wishing to be back at their desks in some fluorescent-lit cubicle in Washington, the next fatherly as they peered at me over their glasses like a cherub-cheeked fantasy of a newshound. Whether they shrugged or smiled, the cynicism of experience colored every action. They'd been coming to the puppet show for 30 years, been behind the stage, and seen the strings go limp when the puppets were returned to their boxes between acts.

The younger reporters mostly appealed to me as a friend. Some were sympathetic—fellow 30-year-olds looking to connect within the bubble of predominantly older, paunchy men. Some used that commonality to disarm me, to try to glean some inside information or anecdote that would appear shortly thereafter in a magazine story. One journalist once padded up to the staff cabin to play cards with me. She was beating me soundly and I didn't stop to wonder why she took the wins with such casualness. We were almost finished playing when I looked up and followed her gaze to the curtain to the front of the plane, which was left slightly parted. Beyond it, you could see the candidate playing his guitar. I realized he'd been there the entire time. Whether she lost her hand didn't really matter; she had won the game. This small detail would appear in print the next day. I'm sure the praise she received from her editors for getting a coveted piece of color outweighed whatever guilt she might have felt from using a questionable tactic to obtain it.

Caught in a precarious place where living, working, and reporting collided, it was never clear what was on the record and what was off, and the two often merged in reporters' minds no matter what they promised. I too conflated my personal relationships with the fact that I was part of the world they'd been assigned to cover.

As a fledgling filmmaker who was interested in capturing a subject's essence—their core, some humanity—I could neither condemn nor excuse the young journalist. It wasn't my place to judge either way. For her, the man behind the curtain with the guitar was more real than he was in public, giving the same stump speech he'd given in front of the same banner just an hour before.

I came to like many of the reporters and journalists personally and to have great respect for their desire to get the facts and stories correct. But there were other aspects to the media's omnipresence that I found more difficult to navigate. One of the hardest things to watch was reporters I had come to know and respect being "spun." I gathered a new appreciation for the aptness of the term *spin*: a point of view or position could take on a life of its own and set off across the media landscape, gathering momentum like a spinning top, if it were charged with the right amount of energy. What exactly that energy was, what made one position or attitude take hold and another die, is still unclear to me.

The spinning accelerated, reaching nausea-inducing speeds as we headed into the summer and my father gathered enough delegates to become the presumed Democratic candidate. And as if spun out of air, we ended up with an oversimplified caricature of each candidate, neither one entirely fair or correct. The absence of a true portrait of either man robbed the country of having a real choice in the election. President Bush came across as the confident, fun-loving, occasionally tongue-tied guy, whereas my father was portrayed as the boring, elitist intellectual with whom you didn't want to have a drink. These caricatures made me wonder what the president was actually like. I watched my father closely and imagined the president's habits and the possibility that he actually had moments of introspection. I knew the images and impressions of my father were so contradictory to his true self that each man must have been suffering from equal frustration. Ironically, my most familiar images of my father were as much of him hunched over a speech, counseling somebody over the phone, as hanging out with his windsurfing friends, in a frayed jean jacket, laughing at their off-color jokes.

To some voters, the presidential election was a popularity contest. Vote for the cool, confident guy you want to hang out with. I couldn't help but think that the media, as a whole, showed little confidence in the ability of the American people to make up their own minds. That every journalist I met during the campaign had an amazing grasp of the issues made me even more confused about the media's seeming inability to simply deliver the facts and let people make their own educated decisions. It seemed clear to me that the issue was not about whose personality was "better," but rather what each candidate, once elected, would do with his power, what policies he would enact, how those policies would affect ordinary Americans, and who was more qualified, tempered, and intelligent.

If this sounds like a criticism of the role the media has come to play in politics, I suppose in part it is. But it isn't a personal indictment of any one decision by any one reporter or news organization. Rather, as someone who has watched intelligent people lose their perspective, I wonder at what distant place the pressure system developed and how it gathered enough strength to get us to this point, where it seems that the news is as capable of obscuring the truth as reporting it.

I remember sitting down for a brief conversation with one of Al Gore's daughters to discuss the campaign process. It was still early on, and she asked how I was finding life in "the bubble."

"What?" I asked. I had no idea what she meant.

She looked at me knowingly. "If you don't know, you're not in it yet."

The "bubble" is the protective space a candidate exists in, not by design, but by natural evolution. At a certain point, usually when a candidate officially becomes the nominee of his party but sometimes before, the accumulated staffers and advisors and the tightly controlled schedule necessary to maintain the pace of campaigning gets the final addition of Secret Service protection. This group of people, clustered loosely around the candidate and swelling naturally to envelop whoever enters, seals off the outside world. There is a deep irony in this. Just when it becomes most important to connect with voters and average Americans, simple logistics make it harder to do so.

The bubble has both physical and abstract aspects. There is the plain fact of having secured perimeters that ensure that no one has casual access to the candidate. And there is the development of the cult of the advisor, which the press loves to report on. While I had been surrounded by them all of my life, I had never really watched advisors and consultants at work up close before. I admired their tenacity, focus, and genuine concern for the future of America. I admired that they were about results; it was the end that mattered, not the means. But sometimes when the end is all that matters, you lose touch with the fact that it is the means that gets you there. Many consultants and paid advisors admitted to me that they lacked legitimate loyalty because the campaign is a job for them and they depend on their reputations to get work. Therefore, some of those on my father's campaign, concerned about their own futures, found it easy to be critical of the campaign and sometimes attempted to blame others for the mistakes and in the end the loss rather than reflecting on how they might have been implicated. Some of these consultants, for instance, assert that they are populists who stand for "the people," but when you read their books or articles, they appear not to have the slightest idea of who "the people" really are. Post New Hampshire, many people were integrated into the campaign from other camps, bringing with them different priorities and loyalties. They often showed a better understanding of props than people. Some are truly brilliant strategists possessing an intuitive sense of political strategy that borders on the psychic. With so many competing voices in the air, the bubble's tendency to make those inside it unable to take a step back and get any sort of sweeping perspective of the campaign landscape can cause candidates to make strategic decisions that to those on the outside seem ill conceived. They are inside the bubble.

Reporters who left our bubble for a week to follow the Bush campaign returned with the same conclusion: With emotions high on both sides and building, in this election cycle, no one was staying home wondering whether there was anything worth voting for. Outside rallies, savvy political propaganda vendors had learned to offer buttons and bumper stickers opposing and supporting the candidate. The demonstrations were issue-based—for every issue imaginable, including that of a lone LaRouchie determined to win converts to his conviction that Dick Cheney was the "beastman," apparently an incontro-vertible fact that was being ignored by the mainstream media.

Global warming activists, angry at the media for ignoring the Bush administration's dismal record on an issue they begged to have covered, demanded to know, for example, why news anchor Jim Lehrer had asked only a single question on the environment when moderating a recent presidential debate. Jim Lehrer was supposed to be on our side, one insisted.

A preteen recruit came dressed up as a space shuttle to get attention for the Apollo Alliance energy-independence-and-clean-alternatives campaign being run by environ-mentalists. Activists fighting AIDS in Africa brought their own signs urging support for legislation; they were the first up to the microphones at most of the town hall meetings. After my father engaged them in a back-and-forth at a rally, elaborating on his Senate ef-fort with Tennessee Republican Bill Frist to address global vaccine shortages, I saw him being counseled by an aide for departing from his stump speech. My father had seen a homemade sign about AIDS in the audience, and he'd responded naturally. These were the spontaneous and organic but dangerous moments when a candidate might be caught off-guard and unwittingly say something that could explode into scandal in the next news cycle.

It was hard to mix the necessary ingredients of caution and passion in the right amounts, particularly for my father, whose instinct was always to dive headfirst into a discussion or conversation. Those closest to him knew not to start a conversation about something important unless we were willing to hang around for a while—he had seeming-ly endless stamina for subjects that captured his interest. It wasn't easy for him to stick to sound bites and the repetitive, simple phrases of the stump speech. His instinct, which wasn't always the best one according to his advisors, was to allow for the complexities of the issues. At times it seemed that the advisors were right, when the press seized on these complexities and portrayed them instead as contradictions.

Away from the positioning, there were the overwhelming crowds. I looked away when I saw grown men sobbing as they tried to give my father their Purple Heart or Bronze Star to carry for good luck. These were privileged moments that didn't belong to anyone other than the candidate and the stranger who embraced him.

People who'd been through a number of campaigns said the level of grassroots pas-sion they were seeing was unrivaled in their memory. The usual pace of a campaign's buildup increased rapidly. Uneasiness about national security probably played a large part. At the time of the 2004 campaign, "security moms" had supposedly replaced "soc-cer moms" out of fear over the next terrorist attacks—which were imminent, according to some political analysts. When those attacks came, as the spin had it, they would certainly be the Democrats' fault for emboldening the terrorists. In every venue, conversations inevitably turned to whether our nation's greatness came from its overwhelming military strength, or whether our weakness was exhibited by our participation in a dubious war that had alienated much of the world and seemed destined for failure.

The intensity of the emotions around this issue manifested in a Mardi Gras-like showmanship at times. Though I still wasn't comfortable with crowds, these characters in their elaborate homemade costumes proclaiming obscure stances were too interesting to ignore. I ventured farther toward the fringes at rallies and other public events, seeking out people who wore their beliefs on their bodies to record with my camera. The camera made me feel anonymous, and I didn't think twice about asking questions when I stood behind it.

"What are you dressed up as?" I asked a couple of people in costume at a rally. They were wrapped in giant flat pieces of foam.

"Flip-flops," one of them said.

My father had been addressing a veterans group in West Virginia when a heckler asked why he had voted against funding for the troops. He explained that he had wanted to vote for the funding, but only if the Senate passed an amendment paying for the war by reducing the tax cuts for the rich and setting out an alternative plan. He voted for the amendment but when it failed, he voted against the overall funding. "I actually did vote for the $87 billion before I voted against it," were his exact words, which were unfortunately obscure. That was it. The opposing side's spin machine took hold of the awkward phrasing and the fruits of their successful labor stood before me, dressed as summer footwear.

"Why are you here protesting?" I asked, curious about what would motivate someone to wake up in the morning, dress up as a symbol in nonbreathable foam, and join a rally in the stifling summer heat.

Instead of answering, one of the flip-flops looked at me. "We know who you are," he said, eyeing me. The other one spat at my feet.

A confrontation like this didn't rattle me as much as the fact that as a nation we allowed our attention to be focused on the deliberate misinterpretation of a response to a badgering heckler instead of on the reality of what was happening on the ground in Iraq in 2004.

That the election was being conducted during a time of war, and in part as a referendum on the justness of that war, had particular resonance because of my father's experiences in Vietnam and afterward, in his earliest experiences with politics as a veteran and war protestor. In our house, my father's experiences in Southeast Asia were notable more for the absence of discussion about them. This was also the case in the houses of my uncles and the other veterans whom I knew well. They did not talk about it. Whatever motivated this silence, it grew to carry a weight of its own over the years, relieved only by a passing or oblique reference every five years or so, a small anecdote never placed into its larger context. I don't know if the whole story was too much for them, or if it was too harrowing or too sacred to share. I only know that it was shared most often through silence—a predicament for a candidate who would soon be encouraged to lean increasingly on his war experience to demystify him as a candidate, to correct erroneous information about his war records, and to help people understand what had driven him into politics.

Although the details of his service in the jungle remained obscure to me, from earliest childhood I knew that Vietnam represented a crucial period in my father's life. I grew up getting to know his brothers-in-arms from Vietnam, including my uncle David Thorne and men who had fought with him on his swift boat, like David Alston. As I grew older, I met men like Senators Max Cleland and Bob Kerrey, who had shared his experiences in war. All of them viewed their decision to come home and oppose the war to have stemmed from the same core of patriotism that led them to go to Vietnam in the first place.

Given that background, I had forgotten that there were Vietnam veterans who had watched the antiwar protests with anger, some of whom would later rally behind the political group Swift Boat Veterans for Truth. My father's testimony against the war before the United States Senate made him a villain in the eyes of people who thought of Vietnam as a winnable war that had been abandoned by weak civilian leaders and a fickle American public. Some people believe a good soldier never disagrees with his superiors because it violates one of the central sacred tenets of the military: the chain of command. In addition, many felt an abiding sadness over how many returning Vietnam veterans had been mistreated by a public that had turned against the war and took it out on the soldiers themselves. This mistake has informed America's approach to war protest ever since. Now the repeated message is, I oppose the war, but I support the troops.

My dad had volunteered to be a soldier, and he loved, respected, and admired the men he had fought alongside. He did not come to oppose the war casually; he did so because his firsthand experiences had caused him to believe that the lives of those men he so admired were worth more than the questionable reasons for continuing the conflict.

Still, if politics has taught me anything, it is that pragmatism is necessary. It is imperative to separate the symbol of "the candidate" from the living, breathing man. The private entity must retain his humanity and withstand constant and deliberate dehumanizing, both by those in his own camp who want to make him more easily understandable and by those in the opposition who seek a means to tear him down. The process of turning a man into a symbol or an archetype is a crucible of sorts, with certain parts of his history or personality being stripped away to reveal a streamlined version. It was essential not to be emotionally affected by it, essential not to take it personally. It was all part of taking a real life and turning it into a winning story.

We crave labels and structure, and campaigns provide narratives that help to assuage that need of voters. These narratives pit traditional American values and beliefs against each other—community versus rugged individualism, for example, was the dominant divide of the pre-9/11 era. The process tends to shoehorn candidates—real people with real lives—into the straitjackets and conformities of these choices. Subtleties and nuances in complex policy positions are shaved down so that one candidate becomes the voice of freedom and peace, the other of order and militarism. My father's campaign was a fascinating case study in myth and ritual. It seemed impossible to me that one person could come to embody an entire system of values and beliefs, especially when we were trying to keep in mind that we should also think of the candidate as an individual.

In a presidential election, candidates become larger than life. They become symbols of hope and opportunity, of strength and faith. Out of a kind of human necessity, people mythologize them, turning an individual into an archetype who embodies a belief system. Their biographies, their childhoods, their college years, and their families come to represent a preordained trajectory that inevitably led them to serve or rescue a nation in need. The most effective parable is the one of suffering and salvation. The candidate overcomes some early trials in life but ultimately succeeds. Each story is poll-tested and then trotted out for one purpose or another during the campaign.

Ghosts haunt the process. The spirits of John F. Kennedy, Michael Dukakis, George H. W. Bush, and Ronald Reagan are ceaselessly summoned by the national media. Myths and stories about past leaders condition the public to the voices of the candidates. Old images are used to create new images, and historic rituals are called upon to produce emotional states. Myths and metaphors permit people to live in a world in which the causes are simple and neat and the remedies easily accessible.

While all this played out in some abstract space occupied by the national media, on the ground the energy grew. Some reporters on the plane said not to trust the size of the crowds as a measurement of anything. The younger of these reporters had seen the crowds at the Dean campaign's "Sleepless Summer Tour" events morph into larger and larger numbers. Then, without warning, the campaign had nose-dived in Iowa—and the crowds had disappeared. The more seasoned veterans had seen the huge crowds that had greeted George McGovern in the weeks before his landslide loss to Richard Nixon. Usually when a candidate has a sympathetic moment on TV or lands an especially powerful line in a debate, pundits call the spike in the candidate's standing a bounce. The journalists speculated that the large crowds at our events might be nothing more than a "dead cat bounce"—meaning that even a dead cat bounces if dropped from a great height.

The gruesome imagery faded as we won state after state on Super Tuesday, with homemade signs, an army of sore feet, days spent waiting in the wilting sun, countless urgent pleas, and a pile of good luck charms that an oversize suitcase could barely contain. Our momentum made the evening of Super Tuesday less surprising, so it felt less impactful than previous primaries, but it was the night that the party coalesced. The following morning, my father called Jim Johnson, one of his senior advisors, and asked him to spearhead the vice-presidential search.

I stood on stage and looked out into the lights again. After a couple of waves and smiles, when you are the background scrim, your mind starts to wander. I watched the celebrating crowd, searching their faces for an anchor. I longed for my mother's perspective. She always had a pointed, wise word that protected us, even my father, from being drawn into the surrealism of the spin. But her world couldn't have been farther away.

5

THE CONVENTION

Many talked about how appropriate it was that the Democratic nominee was formally accepting the nomination in his hometown. For me, it was simply strange to see Boston transformed into a spectacle. The Fleet Center in Boston was almost unrecognizable. Its apotheosis was underscored by the complex security arrangements. Even though I entered the convention hall in the company of the police, there were tense moments when my identity was questioned and my video cameras checked for hidden weapons. This was the first national political convention since September 11, but it wasn't until much later that I realized how deeply the grip of fear had come to influence our politics.

The convention was a riot of images. The floor of the Fleet Center shifted constantly. During the afternoon, little-noticed figures spoke at the podium, ignored by the sparse audience of carpenters, electricians, sound engineers, and camera crews preparing for the real show after dark. In the evening, the hall filled up completely. Technicians faded into the background, and delegates and political alternates assumed their places at the center of the auditorium.

Teachers, union activists, and longtime party operatives, the committed who cared deeply about politics and civic engagement, organized with the chaotic enthusiasm of a circus parade. Nearly every person had paid his or her own way to Boston. Even though the nomination had been decided four months earlier in the eyes of the public and the press, these dyed-in-the-wool activists who gathered at the national convention every four years observed their symbolic role in determining the official candidate of the Democratic Party with great seriousness. They knew the campaign could not go forward, the money could not be spent, and the ads could not be cut until they performed the ritual laying on of hands. Like the Iowans who savored the moments after the doors at a caucus site slammed shut, the delegates relished their experience. They had the last word about the nomination.

Supporters came to the Fleet Center dressed for ritual, bedecked in buttons and ribbons and wild colors—some even painted their faces like football fans do— bearing homemade donkey hats and handwritten signs. There was a sense of freedom and celebration in the air, both liberating and overwhelming, as small-town volunteers mixed with Washington professionals. Gone were the orderly moments of the rope line, the discreet interactions with individuals. Now, everything was a tumultuous wash of sight and sound.

My only regret was that I couldn't be part of the crowd and interact with people as much as I wanted to. By then, I was no longer camouflaged, and many of them recognized me on sight and treated me with either surprisingly intimate enthusiasm or the exaggerated respect and detachment accorded to a member of the prospective First Family. Moving amid them I was simultaneously more vulnerable and more secure—even when released from the bubble, I carried its residual distance with me wherever I went.

I was led onto the ground floor to the sounds of the PA system being tested in the Fleet Center's massive main room. It would later be filled with bodies, but it was empty now, and the sound echoed in the space. The man rehearsing was the public address announcer, whose booming introductions of key moments were noted in the script as V.O.G.—meaning Voice of God. The same role had often been played on the road during campaign events by Marvin Nicholson, my father's mild-mannered and trusted "body man" who walked him through crowds, holding his pen, and guarding him more closely than the Secret Service. Today, the voice was disembodied. Like much of the rest of the campaign, the announcements were more professional, less intimate, while the number of people participating in the process grew larger by the day.

I discovered another, subterranean convention in the catacombs of the Fleet Center, where I went to center myself and rehearse my own brief convention speech. There were no donkey costumes or painted faces there; the standard dress was jeans. In contrast to the carefully constructed trappings of the Fleet Center, the furnishings backstage were spartan, consisting of metal folding chairs and thrift-store card tables that strained beneath the weight of ravaged buffet spreads of junk food. Security people punctuated the dorm-room atmosphere. They were stationed at every turn in the labyrinth, examining the plastic-coated credentials hanging around our necks like armed hall monitors. Never making eye contact, balancing care with a sense of boredom, a seen-everything professionalism, they were a reminder that in spite of all the trappings of revelry, important business was taking place.

The backstage operatives were a band of convention professionals who came together every four years. Their jobs, as speechwriters, scriptwriters, schedulers, speaker trackers, production specialists, makeup artists, mediators, and fixers, were remote from that of the delegates, whom they regarded in a way similar to how a film director thinks about "extras." Their job was to make sure that nothing interfered with the magic hour of prime-time coverage the television networks grudgingly agreed to provide.

I learned this personally when I rehearsed my own speech, in a room named "Celtic" because it was located in a small corner of what was normally the locker room for Boston's professional basketball team.

Sequestered there, I sent revisions and modifications back and forth to some writer friends in Los Angeles. I trusted their understanding of arc and rhythm and knew that they understood the importance of connecting to an audience on an emotional level. We had endless discussions about the nuanced differences among word choices. I wanted to say something that sounded both organic to me and appropriate to the occasion, but it was hard to come up with a narrative that didn't lapse into high-flown rhetoric or meaningless banter. Finally, we whittled down my original version into a carefully proscribed 4-minute package.

But then the rehearsal engineers announced that word had come down from on high that my speech could only be 3 minutes. I had the impression that this sudden change was dictated not only by the schedule, but also by a hierarchy of deals cut with dozens of speakers about their time on camera. Ironically, since they wanted a shorter speech, the one moment that would later receive attention, an anecdote about my father saving a pet hamster from a watery grave by giving it mouth-to-mouth resuscitation, nearly wound up on the cutting room floor.

To help me cut my speech and listen to me practice its delivery, a cabal of my friends and relatives convened at another rehearsal space, one of the buffet rooms at the Boston Park Plaza Hotel that had been modified with a makeshift podium and teleprompters to mimic actual convention conditions. Beneath the tinkling crystals of the chandelier, we spread cut-up pieces of the speech on the fleur-de-lis pattern of the industrial carpeting and moved amid them on all fours, trying to find a way to lose a quarter of the material. Idle or curious busboys paused in their predinner rounds, leaning against the walls in their starched white uniforms to watch what must have looked like some elaborate, grown-up version of Twister. Finally, after hours of haggling over sentences, the speech was edited. I had been focused on the details of the writing process, not on the fact that news organizations representing over 200 countries and 18.3 million viewers would tune in to watch the speech. My friends stared at me as I stood behind the podium and practiced as if it were a college presentation. When I was finished speaking, my friend Colin nodded an affirmation but stared at me with blank eyes.

Because of the tight schedule, I hurried back upstairs to my hotel room to prepare for a tea hosted by prominent female Democrats, one of the many satellite events that absorbed every minute of free time between the convention's activities.

When I arrived at the elevators that went to the floor we occupied, however, I was stopped by the Secret Service members stationed by the elevator doors. I thought one of my friends had been determined a threat, until I realized that I had changed blouses at some point and forgotten to transfer the pin the Secret Service had given to certain members of the staff and family as an unobtrusive badge for security clearance. I searched in vain for a familiar face among their suited ranks, for one of the skeleton crew that had been assigned to our detail earlier. But their jobs required them to be sticklers for protocol; if I didn't have the pin, I wasn't going near that floor.

I was reduced to sneaking through a service entrance and up many flights of a back stairwell. I managed to talk my way past either a more confused or more understanding member of the security team and hurried to my room to change and find the pin. I was both relieved and disquieted that my "mission impossible" had been successful—if I could sneak up a back stairwell, there was the possibility that someone else could, too. In fact, a young LaRouche fan made his way to my room. To our amusement, he stood on a chair and recited his campaign's message.

Pulling myself together for public appearances day after day from a diminishing stock of wrinkled clothing in a suitcase was a challenge; I was constantly discovering that I'd left a shoe beneath the skirt of a hotel bed or that I didn't have the right pair of stockings. Not to mention the added problem that, for the first time in his life, my father had taken an interest in my clothing. "Can you wear something besides jeans?" he'd ask, or frown pointedly at my Converse sneakers. I tried to meet him halfway, knowing that I should make at least some effort to play the part of the political daughter. But the independent streak my parents had so carefully encouraged caused problems. "No, you can't just dress up that vintage shirt by belting it," a friend who had appointed herself my style counselor sighed during one drawn-out wardrobe negotiation.

As my sister and I prepared for national television, I pulled off the dry-cleaner's plastic hoping that my clothes had survived the circuitous two-week trip, and that I could somehow harness the power of makeup to create the magical effect of looking well rested when I was anything but. My boyfriend at the time paced while I sat and waited.

The delegates and other attendees had transformed the Fleet Center. We were urgently navigated to the backstage area through corridors so lively they bordered on chaotic. The show had to run according to a clockwork schedule; not a second of the prime television time would be wasted.

When my turn in the order of speakers came, I focused on the attentive faces of delegates, trying to imagine where they were from and what they did back home, what kinds of journeys had brought them here. I focused on my breathing and put as much volume as I could behind my words. I found the energy to get through it by focusing on the crowd. The rafter-to-rafter rows of color-coordinated red, white, and blue signs conveyed their reactions better than pollster's numbers. In moments of contemplation, the signs waved languidly in the air like underwater fronds. In moments of excitement, the signs rose in unity and pumped the air like some great, energetic machine's multicolored pistons.

The climactic moment of the convention, the one guaranteed to saturate the media coverage, was my father's acceptance speech. The main point of contention during his preparation had been his friend Max Cleland's suggestion, which he ultimately accepted, to begin his address by honoring his Vietnam veteran "band of brothers" by saluting the audience and saying "John Kerry reporting for duty." A conservative with protocol, my father worried that this gesture wouldn't technically be appropriate because he was not an active-duty officer.

His speech was, without question, a reflection of his advisors' decision to elevate him into a mythical figure and a clearly understood "character" by wrapping him in the iconic status of an American Hero. I understood the determination to present him in a context that emphasized why he could be commander in chief. As his daughter, I had private concerns that these presentations—whether the pomp and circumstance or the speeches themselves—could potentially sell my father short by dehumanizing him. Putting someone 75 feet in the air atop a magnificent podium will either bring a candidate closer to us or drive him or her farther away. I wonder if 50 years from now, candidates and viewers will still be enduring this ritual. Maybe we'll make some accommodation to modernity and concede that, in an age of direct, unfiltered Internet communication, when we demand to know everything about everyone, it's anachronistic to introduce our candidates for the highest office in the land in the same way we did when the speeches could be heard only on the radio or, before that, when most Americans would never even hear the sound of their president's voice.

I can't say that I had a bird's-eye view of my father giving his acceptance speech, unless the bird was a barn swallow. During most of the speech, I was crouched on a stairway leading up to the podium area, poised to participate in the celebratory scrimmage that takes over the stage during the cheering and climactic balloon drop. For some technical reason, the drop did not occur on cue. To make matters worse, the audio communications of the poor soul in charge of that moment of stagecraft were somehow picked up by other receivers and broadcast to a wider audience than intended. His panicked mutterings became cries of hysteria as the balloons stayed tidily in their netting above the stage. Repeatedly urging "Go balloons, go balloons," he erupted into curses as they failed to drop. The recording became a hit in the blogosphere.

The celebration would go on without the balloons as the appointed members of the family and inner circle massed onstage. The idea was that the party's cause and its champion were finally and completely reconciled and merged, preparing the way for the general election crusade. It looked and felt to me like those communal dance scenes that end so many movies, from *Footloose* to *Hairspray*.

I did not realize at the time, however, that this moment marked the end of one drama and the beginning of another. Of course, certain changes in my life over the previous few months should have prepared me. In June 2004, a few short weeks before the convention, I had graduated from film school. I had simple expectations for the ceremony: friends and family only.

My father was now methodically followed at all times by a negotiated accumulation of people known as a "press pool." At my graduation, I had realized that for at least the next five months, this press pool was going to be appended to my family, always within range, always at the edges of the action, with us the moment my father set foot outside of a private, Secret-Service-locked-down area and into public view. As I stood onstage waiting to collect my diploma, I looked out at my family, then over their heads at the milling group of reporters. My education had become a media event. It felt less like rite of passage and more like the theater of the absurd. As my friends' parents entered the ceremony through the gate of a magnetometer, it was hard to see where Hollywood ended and the media spectacle of the campaign began.

One night after the convention, I had drinks in St. Louis with our grizzled press "wrangler," a 44-year-old man who could just as easily have been a wrangler of cows or sheep somewhere in the mountainous west, but who instead had the job of literally rounding up and shepherding the press from bus to bus, event to event. He was rough, sometimes ruthless, but charming and honest as all cowboys I have met are. I asked why we had the "press pool"—whether it was an act of democracy to give each news outlet a voice or was it an example of the tipping point. Why did they need to film even the most benign moments, like a candidate walking into a hotel lobby or a restaurant? I wondered when we had become reality television with camera people covering banal bathroom runs.

Perhaps the proof of his bourbon impelled the press wrangler to be more honest than tactful: "You can thank the Zapruder film for that." He explained that after John F. Kennedy's assassination, the news media—the big-three networks—was reduced to relying on one bystander's home movie of the tragedy. In the aftermath, with all the doubts and the questions and the conspiracy theories, the press concluded that there would have to be a new arrangement. Whenever the president and vice president were within public view, a "pool" of representatives from select news organizations would be within earshot, eyeshot, and camera range. After all, you never know when history will be made.

My father had been at Yale playing in a soccer game when JFK was shot. I hadn't even been born. And yet, 40 years later, we were feeling the tragic fallout. Even the term I'd heard reporters use to describe pool duty—"body watch"—suddenly took on a new and unsettling meaning. The cameras weren't recording because there was anything fascinating about my father and I taking a walk near his hotel. This was the body watch pool—a group of reporters with the duty to capture on film what they never wanted to imagine but had an obligation as journalists to record if it did.

I was seven years old when President Reagan was shot. I had never thought about how that footage was captured on camera, or how it ended up on my television. Now, I realized that the cameramen following our every step carried the weight of the world on their shoulders, and yet they had had the decorum, or maybe the decency, never to share the reason with me.

In morbid moods I sometimes looked at the press pool wondering whether they were about to capture on film the most horrible of nightmares. I thought more about these reporters as the group grew: where they came from, who the new faces were in a press corps that had multiplied from what had seemed like an ominous group of 6 in Iowa to 20 on caucus night to 50 everywhere my father went. After all, the body they were watching was my father's. Having to come face-to-face with his mortality when he was diagnosed with prostate cancer had been hard enough. I couldn't allow myself to fully consider the dangers that went along with the job he was applying for. Presidents become figureheads for ideas, targets for madmen. I saw the toll the breakneck intensity of campaigning was having on his health, with his absolute, single-minded dedication keeping him going when his body wanted to give out. We all fear our parents' mortality. I didn't want to consider my father's vulnerability, and yet the group of men and women trailing us was a constant reminder of it. In a way, the convention's symbolic goal of elevating my father to mythic status had a tangible side. He was no longer just a man, he was a walking target. Every breath, every step became a potential moment in history. It was the comfortable fantasy of my father's immortality that I focused on when in reality the body that most needed watching was my mother's.

As the election neared, navigating the route to a scheduled event became like running a gauntlet. Our vans' bulletproof glass was thick enough to protect us from the shouts of the protestors standing along one side of the street, but it was easy to make out their words in the slow-motion angry contortions of their faces. On the other side of the street, thousands waited patiently in lines to go through the magnetometers to get a view of the candidate and the campaign. Veterans in fatigues came to rally around a Vietnam veteran—one of their own—running for president, while opposite them, men who had fought in the same war raised their signs like swords: "Democrats Are Traitors." If the motorcade passed by too quickly, the two sides were indistinguishable.

I often held my camera up to the window as the protesters shouted, perhaps to fictionalize their presence so I didn't have to personally absorb every body blow. But no matter how hard I tried to remain safely removed, a step or two behind a lens, I could feel the power of their opposition, the furious forces marshaled against us. But it wasn't only the negativity that was difficult to process, that I sought unsuccessfully to shield myself from; the raw emotions the campaign brought out could be intense no matter what side of the political divide a person was on.

There was a vulnerability to some of our volunteers, a sadness that trailed them like a shadow no matter what direction the sun was coming from. It made me feel guilty at times, almost as if we were taking advantage, because their sense of commitment often came from having paid a tragic price. It was as if they were at a campaign headquarters in the predawn hours more out of a commitment to their own personal stories and goals than to any specific candidate.

Scott, from South Boston, had never attended a political rally and had been so outside of the political process that he had never voted. He was a carpenter and a reserve soldier. Before he volunteered for the campaign, he had never volunteered for anything, not even a church bake sale. His brother had been badly injured as a soldier in Iraq, and his mom—who had raised the brothers alone—had lost her job in the summer of 2004. Having seen the effects of political decisions firsthand, Scott decided to get involved in the race for president. His brother, who would never walk again, was recovering at a VA hospital and Scott was paying the bills. Missing work meant missing paychecks, but in spite of this hardship, his family had agreed that he should take a week off to volunteer in Florida.

He had a sodden walk and a bad back, caused by an on-the-job injury that he couldn't afford to treat, but he'd leave flyers at several hundred homes in one afternoon. He could explain to voters who were on the fence why he cared so much, why voting mattered, and why he had dropped everything to help a leader get elected. He'd come back to headquarters exhausted, but with a subtle grin on his face. I could tell that he was in physical pain, but he smiled through it. He called his brother every night to give him an update.

After the election results were in, a campaign advisor told me that Scott had called his brother. In his thick Boston accent, he apologized for not working hard enough, for not reaching out to enough homes, for not covering enough ground. It was as if he felt responsible—a personal burden that, however misguided, part of me understood.

Although I was mostly scheduled do events that didn't take me outside the bubble, there were a few occasions on which a harried campaign staffer handed me a sign and told me to go hold it up somewhere. I remember standing on the highway outside of Cincinnati, Ohio, doing "visibility" on the highway that ran between farmland and the boarded-up windows of the postindustrial city, where people had seen their jobs disappear to India and China in recent years, where people watched their companies erect signs that read "There Is No YOU in Union." It was hardly a population center, the side of the road, but we wanted to reach potential voters who wouldn't be attending a rally or watching the nightly news, but might be driving by. I waved my sign at passing cars, mostly flatbed trucks carrying migrant workers back to the city after a day's work in the fields or on the chemical-laden lawns of gated communities. After being crowded in so many seas of people, it felt surreal to wait during the empty seconds between cars. It might have seemed like a waste of time if you divided the number of hours spent by the number of possible voters who passed. I had sped through these landscapes before, keeping my distance through the bus window, but now I'd traveled through the looking glass and had been dropped in the middle of a long stretch of blacktop. The workers on the backs of those trucks were the ones who shouted loudest in support of our signs.

I covered miles on foot under the New Mexico sun alongside Luis, an immigrant from Mexico who decided that since he could not vote, he would walk with us and keep us company instead. As we feebly followed maps, he guided us through entire neighborhoods of Albuquerque, one street at a time. He even tried to buy our entire group Italian ices from a roadside cart, but a quick-thinking staffer turned down the generous gesture, which Luis no doubt could little afford on his salary as a cab driver in a city of car owners. As we walked, he pointed out the houses and apartments where his relatives lived, proud of the roots they had put down.

At a vast trailer park in central Florida, it began to pour—one of those summer deluges that turns the ground into a mud bath and makes everything disappear in a shimmering curtain of steaming silver falling from the sky. My trip advisor was across the byroad and nowhere to be seen. I squinted into the rain, looking for cover, and saw a hand waving to me through the crack of an open screen door. "Come on, over in here," an elderly African American woman motioned to me. I entered her trailer, soaking wet. Ruth's careful hairstyle was that of someone much younger. It was still shiny black, teased and curled and set and sprayed, frozen in place. She pursed her lips and didn't look at me as she bustled around her tiny kitchen.

"You want tea," she said. It was a command, not a question. I stood there dripping and nodded. She apologized for the state of things in the trailer. Her husband had passed away earlier that year, she explained. They had once lived in a "real home," but she had had to choose medicine over mortgage payments and moved to the trailer after all her options had been considered, tried, and exhausted.

"Now all I got are the magazines," she said, pointing to the stack of tabloids next to the sofa. "You're not selling magazines, are you?" she narrowed her eyes at me suddenly. I shook my head. She went into the bathroom while the tea steeped and returned with a flowered hand towel, which she carefully spread out on her sofa before gesturing to me to sit.

"That'll catch most of the water," she said. "Things don't dry out ever once they get wet in this swampland. I swear I have some laundry been hanging outside for six months." She sighed and passed me a cup. The tea was sweet, much sweeter than I ever would have made for myself, but all the better for it. Ruth looked at her clock and picked up the remote.

"Time for my show," she said, and turned on the television. The familiar theme song for *CSI* came on. Police procedurals were familiar to me since I had started traveling and spending so much time in hotel rooms, but I usually fell asleep as the credits opened.

I settled back on the sofa and let the comforting, orderly pattern of the case unfold. The rain pounded on the roof and water trickled down two of the walls, forming a small puddle in the corner.

"That Stokes isn't as quick as Grissom, is he," she shook her head.

As we chatted idly about the characters on the show, something unspoken moved me; I hope it moved us both. The past month had been hard and exhausting. I realized that this was the first moment of peace I had found, and strangely, I'd found it in the trailer of someone I had just met.

These are the moments that make sense, the still points in the whirling mass of memory. They are the pivot points, the people and places and times when something in me shifted.

6

AUGUST

August has always seemed a transitional month to me. Summer's highlights, the sun so wiltingly hot that when my toes broke the swimming pool's surface, I welcomed the water's icy grip, contrasted with the earliest twinge of the throat-aching melancholy I associate with fall. Daylight stretched impossibly until dinnertime. During 2004, the dog days of late summer resurrected the blend of emotions. The election cycle was at its low ebb, giving the campaign a moment to catch its breath before the full-steam push of fall began.

I spent most of the month trying to reconnect with what remained of my nonpolitical life. I went back to Los Angeles, spent short bursts of time with my friends, and made what efforts I could to pursue the career I had intended to start, taking meetings at film studios and allowing myself to imagine the projects I might take on when I had the time. Most people in Hollywood know that business shuts down in August, but I used the studio meeting ritual as a way to move forward and ground myself in my own life. I took early morning walks in the hills above my house. On the campaign trail, I had become used to, if not always comfortable with, never being alone, so I relished these hours of solitude. I had become so accustomed to the breakneck schedule that I felt some guilt about taking this time for myself, but we had been told that August was downtime for the presidential campaign and the best thing we could do was recharge.

Everybody connected with the campaign was drained. The physical toll of campaigning is something the public rarely sees; so much effort is put into hiding it, into having candidates and surrogates look fresh and energized at every appearance, whether it's the first or the 12th of the day. Privately, we were exhausted. My father had strained his voice so badly in the endless hours of giving speeches that he was under strict doctor's orders not to speak unless absolutely necessary. Conversations with him had become one-way, and he'd convey amusement or disapproval only with facial expressions and whispered one-word answers. In the stillness of my kitchen, I realized that I was vibrating with a constant, nagging feeling of incompleteness, as if I had left my wallet somewhere but couldn't remember when I had seen it last. I tried to breathe into the quiet of the rooms, relishing the facade of the two parties calling a traditional and figurative truce.

If there was ever a good time to rest, it was in those final hot weeks of summer. Under the rules of public financing for the general election, each party was required to use only the finite federal funds provided for the general election from the moment of nomination to election day: For the Democrats this spending countdown started five weeks earlier than the Republicans because of the timing of the conventions. Even our constant companions on the campaign trail, the "bigfoot" Washington political journalists, were escaping the heat at places like Martha's Vineyard, where they sipped drinks and strolled on private beaches while trading insights about what was best for the country.

I tried to pick up the threads of what remained of my private life and realized I was so far behind on so many aspects of my friends' lives that what was needed would be more accurately described as starting over than catching up.

I practiced the word "remission" over and over as if it were part of a speech. I wasn't certain how it sounded or if I trusted its implications. My mother was celebrating her second month of being cancer-free. The doctors never used the word "cured." A patient isn't allowed that relief until five years without an episode. And while I tried to believe when the doctors said things like, "We're on course with the expectations of the results of the expected course of action," their tone and the doublespeak of their message left the same empty feeling that the carefully crafted vanilla-bland branding vocabulary of the national campaign did. I had to occasionally remind myself in both cases that somewhere behind the language was a person.

Sitting with friends in front of my TV in LA, nursing cup after cup of green tea followed by the occasional late-night whiskey, I watched the talking heads on television endlessly prognosticating, pontificating, lecturing, yelling at one another, and in some cases rising to competing screams in fervent attempts to explain "what would happen." It was all nothing more than a televised shamanistic ritual, a throwing of the bones dressed up with suits and sets that looked like conference rooms. None of them had any idea. They sneered at each other's crystal balls and read out predictions that seemed no more plausible than those delivered by horoscopes. And when the media had exhausted its seers, they turned to another standby: polls. They conducted polls on what viewers wanted to watch, on what viewers thought was going to happen, on how viewers felt the media was doing with its polls. Meanwhile, the campaigns were also conducting polls on what the viewers wanted to hear. They sat side-by-side in newsrooms or on beaches and informally negotiated what the rest of the country would spend the next year being told was important and relevant.

I became adroit at skirting around the edges of my doubts. After living in dislocated spaces and moving at such high velocity through heightened anxiety and states of the unknown, I projected onto my mother's recovery the perhaps immature hope of what I wanted to be true: that her healing and prognosis meant everything would be fine. People get sick, they die in car accidents every day; I was lucky to be dealing with just a little cancer and a run for the presidency—it was not that abnormal. Even the drama of her illness had somehow worked its way into my new narrative. I had become so strangely comfortable in the netherworld of information relay that I relied on reports delivered under fluorescent lights and statistical projections instead of my gut. On my walks, when the wind hit my neck in a strange way or emotional observations about what illness does to the body and the mind haunted me, I replaced the chill with uncharacteristic logic.

The end of the summer is traditionally a time for virtually everything in American life but politics; presidential campaigns formally begin on Labor Day. Most Americans were watching the Olympics, vacationing, reading, and getting their kids ready for another school year. Even in an era of relentless campaigning and media overload, August seemed like a time of rest. We were lulled by the traditional timetable into a false sense of security.

I was in Hawaii for a friend's wedding on August 4, the day the first ads appeared. Bored by the monotony of being on the treadmill in my hotel's gym, I looked up as my father's face flashed on four television screens that hung from the ceiling, blocking any view of the ocean. I was used to being constantly surrounded by the surrealism of his two-dimensional image by then—every gate in the airports I walked through had television sets tuned to CNN, delivering the constant banter of the campaign—but something about the footage caused me to turn down the music in my headphones so I could hear the story. It was about advertisements being run by a seemingly obscure fringe group that called itself Swift Boat Veterans for Truth. The first ad featured a series of men claiming to have personal knowledge that John Kerry had "lied" about his war wounds and his war record and "betrayed" his comrades in Vietnam.

Four different channels commented on the same attack. Even with the knowledge that the networks were trying to ensure they didn't get scooped by singling out the same news item, there was an edge to the newscasters' voices that echoed as I listened to my friends talk about their babies and their jobs later that day at the wedding.

There were no real details and no documentation, just faces and incendiary charges. New ads appeared later in the month, shifting from vague attacks on my father's war record to angry and inaccurate characterizations of his 1971 testimony before the Senate Foreign Relations Committee after returning from Vietnam, in which he questioned the morality and winnability of the war and the unwillingness of the Nixon administration to admit to the American people that it had given up on victory.

In the middle of the month, the conservative Regnery publishing house came out with a book, *Unfit for Command: Swift Boat Veterans Speak Out Against John Kerry*, that retold the same distorted views. The Swift Boat Veterans for Truth's leader, John O'Neill, who had been trying to discredit my father since 1971, was its purported author.

My first instinct was to laugh it off. The ads were paid for and produced by a handful of conservative ideologues. They featured "testimony" from a small group of Vietnam vets who had spent decades bitterly arguing that America should have fought in Vietnam forever if that was how long it took to "win."

We waited, lulled by the impression that the advertisements' clear bias and inaccuracy would ensure their rapid fall off the radar and out of the news cycle. We were wrong. The attacks did matter because they fed an entirely new media beast. The big newspapers investigated the ads' claims and found them wildly inaccurate, but fewer and fewer voters read newspapers for political information. Moreover, the vast majority of Americans who relied on television for such information no longer depended on the objectivity of a handful of trusted anchors to tell them what was legitimate news. The idea of "balance" had been perverted into a tit-for-tat back and forth between news outlets with varying degrees of bias. *CBS Evening News* anchor Dan Rather lost his job in part over his *60 Minutes* report on Bush's National Guard service that had a few of the facts wrong but the fundamentals correct, and yet nothing happened to the Fox News reporters who endlessly trumpeted the Swift Boat Veterans' ads' false claims about my father's Vietnam record. It should have been very simple: This group is airing some ads, their claims are not true, end of story.

But the timing of the ads was, objectively speaking, strategic genius. Like a midnight ambush, an attack timed for August benefited from an ever-growing and ever-hungrier news consortium of television networks and other media outlets idling in frustration until September. They pounced on the shred of story and began to inflate it to fill the empty hours and pages.

Blogs are omnipresent now, and it seems strange to say that until that August, I knew little about them. The genre was in its infancy then, and 2004 would be the first national general election in which blogs would play a significant part. During the 2008 primary between Barack Obama and Hillary Clinton, they were the source of "reliable" information constituents looked at first. That summer, they played a nascent but essential role. The conservative bloggers' main political function was to keep political stories alive long after the mainstream news media might have discarded them. They reinforced attack lines by sheer force of repetition, however untrue they might have been. Unlike bigfoot journalists, bloggers eschewed the traditional "gentleman's news cycle"; they did not take vacations, did not view August as downtime, did not even appear to sleep. In conjunction with the cable talk shows, they made the outrageous claims seem like news, and then the ads themselves became news. Then the discussion of the ads became news, with the news reporting on itself.

In 2004, we also failed to appreciate the effectiveness of the "fear and smear" festival masquerading as the Republican National Convention. The Democratic National Committee had been careful to avoid resorting to such tactics at our own convention, in part because in surveys and focus groups, undecided voters had said they deplored partisanship and negative attacks on the opposition. Our convention's speakers had been strongly urged not to even mention, much less attack, the president, to avoid bashing Republicans and in general to accentuate the positive. Politics was about optimism, not negativity, we had felt instinctually and had been told by countless consultants. Focus on the future, not the past, they had said. Ad hominem attacks and character assassinations simply discredited the attacker, they reasoned. Barack Obama, for example, gave a speech that not only launched him onto the national stage but also was hailed by many as an important postpartisan treatise.

Given the example the Democrats had tried to set in Boston, it came as a shock when Georgia Democratic senator Zell Miller launched into a diatribe at the Republican convention attacking a national security record, based on stale, flimsy "analysis" of votes cast decades in the past. And New York governor George Pataki and New York City mayor Rudy Giuliani harnessed the still-raw emotions aroused by September 11 to beat up the opposition. But perhaps I was naïve to expect otherwise from a team that journalists said had perfected the politics of personal destruction.

7

ELECTION COUNTDOWN

There were days when the temperature rose to 105°F, the air-conditioning broke, and I sat in my chair at a rally or "front porch" event, soaked with sweat. There were evenings when it seemed it might never stop raining, and three pairs of tights under my jeans did nothing to stave off the fear that the air itself might freeze. And yet we were propelled forward. The bags were in the van. The van was waiting. Another plane to catch.

At airports, I felt strangely free. I loved the anonymity of airport corridors, the characters and cultures that swept by in my peripheral vision. Divorced from context, faces took on immediacy and urgency.

A plastic-cushioned chair with a shared armrest beckoned at the gate marked "Tulsa, Oklahoma." I had to resist the urge to settle in to watch and guess who was going away on a business trip or returning home, whether someone would greet them at the airport, whether they were on their way to a funeral, or to the kind of vacation I so craved. But I always kept moving.

Identifying the familiar texture of each state's geology from the plane's windows reminded me of long car rides when I was young, when we tried to spot a license plate for every state. The game could go on almost endlessly on the highways of Massachusetts; the roads were always crowded with cars from Connecticut, Maine, Vermont, and New Hampshire. Someone's visiting grandparents likely accounted for a plate from Florida, and their orange lettering was enough to induce fantasies of an endless summer, even on the dreariest days.

I traveled through 33 states, like in the grown-up equivalent of the license-plate game.

In New Hampshire and Iowa, I'd noticed the nuances of the landscape and its inhabitants, but as the campaign escalated, the landscapes seemed as indistinct as anonymous cars passing on the highway.

The entire experience began to feel like an experiment engineered by Lewis Carroll—a small country became big, only to shrink down again. At first, we'd navigated the landscape by motor vehicle, ticking by the miles visibly on the odometer, and then by jumbo jet, racking up thousands of frequent flier miles. In the end, we returned to a ground game of highways and bus caravans. After New Hampshire and Iowa came the mountains of Colorado, the desert of New Mexico, the Great Lakes of Michigan, the boardwalks of the New Jersey shore. In the closing months, the country was miniaturized again, to what felt like exclusive headquarters in Ohio.

In Iowa on caucus night, my father had said he loved Iowa, and he had repeated that same sentiment about New Hampshire a week later. He was not speaking just of the love of victory. These states had become second homes to him and the intrepid souls who had joined him on the campaign. He was saying, "I know your state," and every head in those ballrooms had nodded because they had known exactly what he meant.

In the general election, we were like novice readers in the speed-reading course. The time spent getting comfortable in the early states simply cannot be replicated when the whole process speeds up and six Iowa towns in a day becomes six key states in a day.

Trapped in the bubble that now contained a 60-member traveling press corps, a dozen staff members, and a cadre of Secret Service officers, there was no idle stopping at the farm stand to choose a few ears of corn, bright orange pumpkins, or bumpy gourds. There were instead sterile, clockwork encounters when the motorcade stopped, the cameras raced into position, and the candidate walked over to pick up a container of strawberries, sample the local Wisconsin cheddar, or try the blue-ribbon-winning fudge. Advance staffers sat on pins and needles, fearful that the warm old gentleman behind the counter would decide that this was his moment to give the Democratic nominee a piece of his mind about high taxes or socialist medicine. Secretly, this was something I waited for: a true voice breaking through, puncturing the managed quality of so many of the events.

Occasionally, unscripted life would sneak in the invariably comic spectacle. I remember once in Wisconsin when the advance team informed us that we were actually ahead of schedule and would arrive early at the next event—a virtually unprecedented occurrence. The caravan pulled over and the entire campaign staff piled out of the buses and cars to play an impromptu game of touch football in an empty field across the street from a housing development. The pile of temporarily discarded sportjackets grew as shirtsleeves were rolled up, and the grueling routine of the workday was temporarily suspended with all the thrill of a spontaneous midday fire drill. Men ran the cross patterns of their youth and called urgently for the ball.

Suddenly an elderly man in a bathrobe appeared, crossing the street from a house at the edge of the development. He looked angry and astonished as he pulled the terrycloth belt more tightly around his waist.

"What is going on here?" he asked, looking around to try to make sense of all the cars and the grown men running giddy zigzags in the normally empty lot outside his window. He eyed everyone suspiciously; clearly, he recognized no one. Whatever hobbies or distractions he had in his life, they kept him from this piece of news that defined our universe. The man sputtered and rubbed his eyes while my father backpedaled in the tall prairie grass, going long for one last pass.

Those days were the last limping yards of the marathon. When the alarm rang, I was certain I'd had only 3 minutes of superficial sleep, and I had to drag myself out of bed. Struggling with the coffee maker in my hotel room seemed as difficult as performing major surgery. I'd step over the newspapers, which lay at the threshold like flagstones. I dreaded the newspaper less in those later days because the pictures and headlines alternated news of wins and losses daily.

The reporters became possessive about certain hotel chains, not just for the hotel club points they were accumulating for postcampaign vacations, but for the merits of one chain's beds over another, a preference for the Westin coffee over the Marriott's tea. They became creatures of habit, relying on the uniformity to keep them sane as daily deadlines quickened and the one deadline that counted most—the election itself—loomed with great uncertainty.

The plane's wheels bounced to a stop on the tarmac surface, and my father bounded down the steps in the same way as always, hurrying to a bunting-draped hangar to deliver the same concerns to a different audience. Every rally by now looked almost identical: the signs, the bunting, the backdrops, the theater-in-the-round setup that even the grizzled television reporters admit shows up well on television.

The "press file," the gathering spot designated for the local and national reporters who trailed the campaign like the followers of a medieval crusade, was always located in the most cavernous room available. If the rally was at a college, the file was surely the gymnasium; if the rally was outside, the file was a tent, replete with heat lights if we'd touched down in Wisconsin, Ohio, or Minnesota. If we were in Arizona, New Mexico, or Florida, we would see air-conditioning pumps reminiscent of NASA's takeover of the family home in *E.T.: The Extra-Terrestrial*. The press file could be dropped down out of the sky anywhere at any time for either a Republican or Democratic event, and one could not tell the difference between the two.

Another ritual began when a staffer came up with the idea of bringing the outside in, giving the otherwise nondescript press file a taste of the place it was in. Reporters and staffers were soon tripping over each other on their way to the buffet to learn that in Cincinnati, the local chili—first concocted by a Macedonian immigrant in 1922—is served over spaghetti. In Kansas City, an advance staffer with the near-Solomonic task of choosing between local barbecue joints pragmatically compromised by securing takeaway aluminum tubs of the best smoked meat both Gates and Sons' and Arthur Bryant's restaurants had to offer. It's best not to get involved in old-time rivalries when votes are at stake. In Arkansas, tamales, gumbo, shrimp, and even steaks miraculously appeared from Doe's

Eat Place, sending reporters into a downward spiral of nostalgia for the months they had spent in Little Rock. Stone crabs in Miami. Cheese in Wisconsin. Microbrews and tiny gift bags of Starbucks coffee in Seattle.

It was akin to visiting "It's a Small World" at Disneyland and convincing yourself you'd journeyed to another country. Still, it was better than yet another tasteless meal ladled into Styrofoam, and it led the weary travelers to pine wistfully for the freedom they'd enjoy after November 2. They fantasized about returning to Arkansas, Florida, Missouri, Ohio, and driving up without a motorcade or "minders," as the advance team was often called, taking a seat in a worn booth at Doe's, Joe's Stone Crab, Gates, or the Empress, and just having a meal.

In the morning, I would wake up to find my voice husky and ravaged as I piled on the layers I'd need to stay warm at an early morning rally in Illinois. By afternoon, I would be peeling off layers at a rally in Orlando. At the evening event in Madison, Wisconsin, my carelessness in not applying sunscreen had the shivering Wisconsinites wondering how I had acquired an October sunburn.

The air smelled different—brinier—in Seattle, off Elliott Bay, than it did just a few blocks from the Willamette River in Oregon, and different still in Tempe, Arizona, or landlocked locales in the Midwest.

Identical convenience stores at every airport boasted of selling the "Taste of [Fill-in-the-Blank] City," when my only desire was to board the plane and fall into a merciful sleep. Sometimes, though, I wished I was flying home to a waiting family to whom I could bring a local souvenir, be it taffy, sourdough bread, a snow globe, or Oregon wine at insanely marked-up prices.

I learned to close my eyes and let the sounds of the crowds at rallies drift over me, to pick out the different accents in the music of their voices: Pockets of people speaking Spanish, the warmth of a Southern twang, the sharp yet soothingly familiar New England accents at the rally in Portsmouth during the American League play-offs, when hundreds of Red Sox fans in broken-in ball caps cheered. I learned how different states looked as they came into focus from the air, which airports seemed to appear suddenly in the desert, which airports seemed to melt into the mountain terrain, and which seemed to have been planted in the middle of a big city, surrounded by highways glimmering with the headlights of cars inching forward as if they were being carried by a sluggish conveyer belt.

If it was a Sunday, one of our local stops inevitably was a place of worship. Many of the election postmortems suggested that one of the biggest divides between red-state and blue-state America concerns religious faith. Poll after poll demonstrated that non-Latino Caucasians who regularly attended religious services tended to vote for Bush, while those who did not attend were apt to vote for Kerry. In some ways, this "religious divide" was not surprising. There is no question that President Bush's team had a genius for sprinkling biblical references into his speeches to let conservative Christians know he was "one of them." President Bush's chief political advisor, Karl Rove, waxed victorious about how he had urged the use of carefully constructed language to speak to an ever-more-segmented segment of the electorate, and the president's chief speechwriter was well versed in the kind of biblical language that was the president's rhetorical bread and butter.

By comparison, Democrats were wedded to discussing programs seemingly forgetting the values—secular and religious—upon which policy is founded. Democrats might discuss the need for better preschool and community programs for underprivileged families, whereas conservatives would frame the conversation in terms of "family values," strategically invoking a set of allusions deeply ingrained in the Western worldview.

On the surface, the voting record of regular churchgoers made sense. But below, beyond the obvious image of the Republicans as the party of the religious and the Democrats as the party of the "godless," the facts were not as clear-cut.

The details or specifics of my father's degree of religiosity are irrelevant to me. I had always appreciated how serious he was about obeying and living by one of Jesus' few direct commands to the faithful: "Do this in remembrance of me." He took this on as a personal responsibility, and it was what he'd speak of at town hall meetings, when I'd hear him cite Matthew 25:40: "Whatever you do to the least of these, you do unto me." My father argued that the ethical test of a good society is how it treats its most vulnerable members. He'd thought deeply about how to translate his faith into protecting the environment, fighting AIDS, reducing poverty. I think the inner struggle he faced as a veteran over what constituted a just or unjust war had a lot to do with his desire to reconcile his faith with the way he lived his life.

Some pundits argued that his relationship with God wasn't something that he felt comfortable using as a campaign device, but I believe what was missing in that analysis was the reality that it wasn't just his own New England steeliness that made him uncomfortable with public displays of piety, it was his faith itself. His thought process allowed the observant to pray quietly and humbly rather than making ostentatious displays. As he said in his convention speech, he, like most Catholics of his generation, didn't wear his faith on his sleeve. But he did wear it beneath his skin, like a sort of internal shield.

The challenge lay in communicating that piety to a suspicious audience. Like the proverbial tree falling in the forest, it was difficult to say with confidence that quiet Catholicism made a sound that voters could hear and trust.

Because my father is a lifelong Catholic, with both religious and cultural ties to the church, one of the most contradictory and painful experiences of the campaign for him was when a handful of bishops suggested that he, the first Catholic presidential nominee since John F. Kennedy, should be denied the obligation to "do this in remembrance" of Jesus by taking Communion because he, like a majority of American Catholics, didn't believe the government should make decisions for women coping with unwanted pregnancies.

If the Catholic Church had carried out this threat and denied Communion to all Catholics who supported a woman's right to choose, it would have been denying it to a majority of congregants. Enforcing this kind of doctrinal strictness raised other inconvenient questions about politicians who voted against the interests of the poor or the environment, both of which were rock-steady positions of a Church deeply committed to the virtues of charity.

For me, the Sunday masses were chances to get away from the campaign. They were peaceful moments to sit and think, listen to singing, or in many cases watch a well-rehearsed show. The hour-long service was a respite from the heat of summer and the frantic campaign, but it was also enough time for opponents and protesters to plaster cars with flyers about abortion rights. As women walked from the church to their cars, fanning their faces with wide-brimmed hats, they learned that Democrats, in their private moments, have a penchant for killing babies, another rung that sent the debate spiraling further downward.

Some in the Church's hierarchy even suggested that Kerry supporters be denied Communion. Seeing religion used in this way seemed sadly ironic. It was Martin Luther King Jr., James Lawson, and John Lewis—preachers and ministers, poets and prophets—who had helped deliver the right to vote to all Americans. Taylor Branch's famous trilogy about the civil rights movement—*Parting the Waters, Pillar of Fire*, and *At Canaan's Edge*—captures the combination of faith, reason, and movement it took to change our society. He charts the direct line from the Old Testament through Jesus and finally to these modern heroes—King, Diane Nash, James Bevel, Bayard Rustin, Lawson, and Lewis—who changed America and made it what it is today.

In churches, I watched in awe as people sang hymns and gave thanks for rivers crossed and acknowledged long journeys ahead. Though I was raised with a religious father, I was not particularly devout and had decided to go to church only occasionally, as part of the Christmas ritual. I was amazed by the strength of the faith of the people across the country especially on a Sunday morning. The personal is political and, for many, the personal—the way the day begins and ends—has everything to do with their relationship with God.

I was overwhelmed by the hospitality of the congregations of so many churches that welcomed "the tall white girl" into their pews, their hearts, and their homes to share their worship. And I understood why people believed government should reflect what their faith instructs about life and leadership. I sat in a Baptist church that shook with energy and felt what it was like to be in a roomful of congregants who had lost themselves to the emotion of worship.

Later, when I found out that a certain minister had handed out posters saying that voting for Democrats would be going against the will of God, I was amazed that someone charged with acting as a conduit between people and God would be comfortable using his power in such a way. Seeing religious leaders try to strip from their parishioners their right to hold dissenting opinions made me wonder if we've come too far from our origins as a country founded on the separation of Church and State. I questioned my own faith in organized religion when I heard how some people spoke about my father.

I believe in the parable of the Good Samaritan, and yet we were labeled as sinners when we spoke of the need to move toward universal health care rather than relying on the free market to care for the elderly, the sick, and the young. We believed every human being is beautiful in the eyes of God regardless of race, class, or gender, and yet we were told that some of our brothers and sisters were not equal before the law because of whom they loved.

I learned that I should love my neighbor as I love myself, and yet we were called socialists when we asked why interest rates on credit cards for poor people were so high. I learned that I should not be a hypocrite, and yet that is what we were called when we argued that birth control helps women avoid pregnancy, abortion, and deadly diseases such as AIDS. I was taught that Jesus said if your enemy is thirsty, give him water; if she is hungry, bring her food. Apparently that applies only if that enemy is not Muslim. I was taught early on that if someone steals your cane, it is holy to give him your cloak. Yet taxing corporations to feed the homeless is perceived as almost sacrilegious. I was taught that when Jesus was struck, he offered his attacker the other cheek, yet we were told to bless "Shock and Awe" and to stop talking about the windfall contracts given to Halliburton for work in Iraq. I suppose faith is translated in the eye of the beholder or in the heart of the believer, but it was hard to understand how we could have translated our faith in the same God so differently from so many of our critics.

As much as my understanding of my own complicated relationship with faith was tested over those weeks, it was also reaffirmed. In the autumn, while I campaigned alone as a surrogate, I visited a number of Baptist churches. I remember one service in particular at a modern, unassuming church in a small town in Nevada. The building came to life when its congregation filled it. The service was a swirl of sights and sounds and deeply moving experiences—literally moving, because it was impossible to sit still as sound and music swept through the room.

The music was the most obvious novelty to me, not just in the amount of talent among the members of the beautifully robed choirs, but in the congregations themselves. Catholics, however pious, cannot seem to master singing in harmony. The atmosphere radiated through everyone present and was an inspiring reminder that politics really can be about joy and hope.

It brought a brief moment of escape from CNN and the horde of cameras, but what followed was the inevitable collision with reality: Nothing was more sobering than leaving that church and seeing on the windshields in the parking lot those pamphlets instructing the worshippers that they'd be betraying their faith if they voted for a Democrat.

The politics of joy inside the church told one story, the pamphlets outside told another. So did the direct mail sent by the Republican National Committee to voters in West Virginia and Arkansas, warning them that if the Democrats got elected, they would ban the Bible. In several swing states, anti-gay voters were identified and received automated calls that allegedly came from pro-gay groups urging them to vote for Kerry. Elsewhere, all over the country, men dressed in unconvincing drag held up pro-gay signs while hassling voters, pretending to be proxies for the Kerry campaign. All of this—the direct mail, the flyers, and the men in drag—seemed to imply that God is a Republican, when we all know this isn't true—he's a Red Sox fan.

The presidential campaign had taken on the trappings of a crusade on both sides. The people whose passion we encountered seemed to be working and praying for a utopia, for a government and a republic that could vindicate all their hopes and dispel all their fears. But I eventually came to the conclusion that the most devoted partisans in both campaigns thought America already was utopia, in the limited sense of a place where government could not thwart the natural virtue of the people—the place so often described as a "shining city on a hill." And they feared, from their different perspectives, that we were losing the qualities that made us unique and even blessed by God. It was not a battle to be won; it was a battle that was essential not to lose.

I found it sobering to watch the politics of fear triumph over the politics of hope. And it was not the winning or losing that was most dispiriting, it was how the battle was waged. I understand the phrase "nothing is sacred" better now than ever before. Nothing, not even those things that might seem by rights to be above campaigning, is immune from being twisted and turned into a weapon. Even a cross can be a dagger.

In the low moments when it seemed the campaign was only a bitter crusade defined by the urgency with which the American people fought for their sacred values, I turned to the feeling, larger than political affiliation, that had united us all in that hot Baptist church in Nevada.

In contrast, the debates felt like cease-fires. In many ways they were among the most civilized periods of the campaign, with both candidates retreating to their respective corners to prepare for the coming round. The attention of both campaigns was focused inward, on their man and their strategy, causing the usual exchange of fire over the airwaves to disappear. It was the proverbial calm before the storm. There were three presidential debates, each in its own strategic location. In September, we walked on the wide, faded yellow beach in Miami before gathering ourselves for the quiet motorcade ride to the debate. The trip had a certain gravitas. It was as if we were all walking toward that hallowed democratic moment institutionalized by the Greeks, when those who wish to participate in the governing of the state present themselves in front of the populace and articulate their views as clearly as they can. Oratory and debate—the free exchange of ideas—are cornerstones of a government of the people, by the people. Despite the sometimes trite ads and occasional moments that felt like pandering, there was still something noble at the center of this process.

As we gathered for our usual motorcade loading ritual, someone pushed me to the front of the caravan. "You ride with your father," he said. "It will relax him." I knew that some advisors didn't feel this way because I often wore my anxiety on my sleeve; the traditional sin of politics is to display or express a genuine emotion. Aware of the privilege, I tried to do my appointed job and stay calm as I sat next to him, watching the neon lights of Miami blinking behind the exotic shadows of palm trees. He whispered practice answers, and I held my breath. When he scratched a thought on his legal pad, I did not speak.

The first debate was the last debate I sat in the audience for. Feeling plastic-wrapped by the political image I was supposed to uphold, I excused myself halfway through and went searching for my camera, more to distract myself than because of any true sense of mission or deep need to record the event. By the time the moderator, Jim Lehrer of PBS's *The NewsHour with Jim Lehrer,* posed his fourth question to the candidates, I was conveniently lost in the back catacombs with two friends. This was a strategy I would subconsciously adopt from time to time during the later stages of the campaign. When I was actively engaged in a rally or an event, I felt like I was learning and participating, assisting in some way. My thoughts were distracted and occupied by my responsibilities. If I had nothing to do but watch, a certain low-level nervousness that probably was always present became more apparent.

Down the hall from the studio audience, I heard echoing cheers. The muffled sound of celebrating advisors bounced off the cement brick walls as I walked out into the hallway and joined the group as though I had never been missing. It reminded me of a story my friend had told me about arriving late for a 10-K race. She exited the subway, saw the throng of runners passing along the street, and plunged in as if she had been running since the starter gun. I joined just in time to cross the finish line, looking suitably relaxed.

Afterward, the gathering at the hotel was loose and convivial, punctuated by back-slapping and celebratory stories that reached back to people's childhoods. I wouldn't have been surprised to overhear a triumphant tale of someone's performance as a molar in a third-grade health play about the digestive system. The relief of success and the balmy Miami weather thawed personalities. It was a lovely, slightly exotic night that unspooled in the oceanside air.

The next morning, relaxed by celebration and success, we loaded with casual ease into the motorcade. I had earned the seat next to my father again—thanks to those "just to be safe" superstitions that underpinned so many of the decisions made on the fly during the campaign—and climbed inside while he completed a photo spray. We had jumped 10 points in the polls overnight. There was a sense of rejuvenation, of fresh life and vitality.

I called my sister, who had watched the debate in Philadelphia with mothers of soldiers stationed in Iraq. I had not received a congratulatory call from her to pass along yet, nor had I received a call from my mother reassuring me that she was, of course, still in remission. Neither Vanessa or I had attended my mom's scans as they fell on the same day as the debate and she, confident about her health, had encouraged us to remain on the trail. As important as it may have seemed then to be with my father, I realized later that I should have been with my mother. I used the free moments in the car to place a call myself. My sister answered her cell. Her greeting was quick, perfunctory, and to the point. I knew she was busy with her studies, but I was taken aback that she wasn't keen to share the happiness of the preceding night's success.

"Why didn't you call?" I asked.

She hesitated. "Hold on, Mom wants to talk to you."

My mother got on the line. Her voice was soft, a monotone.

"What happened?" I asked.

"My tests weren't very good yesterday," she said.

"What do you mean?" I asked, climbing out of the motorcade SUV. I had to move. I walked across the parking lot with my hand on my chest. No breath. I don't remember exactly what she said, something about three new tumors, her chest, the first tumor replicating into three. No matter what words the doctors chose or how the phrases were organized, the prognosis was not good.

I looked up into the air, hoping that the sky would ground me; looking down was making me spin. To my right, three press buses were lined up, ready to leave, and would yet again be following us as we drove. I caught the eyes of the reporters inside, who stared at me while I paced.

Concentric circles of people surrounded my father—Secret Service officers, advisors, handlers, handshakers. They had never seemed like barriers before, but suddenly, when it was essential to get through them, I felt powerfully the distance they created between us. I had to push through the crowd like the people on the rope line do. I was outside the circles and, with the burden of my news, I was outside the upbeat emotional tone of the moment as well. I had been given a sudden weight I needed my father to help me carry.

"Please get in the car," I said to him. We had 15 minutes to take in the news and make whatever plans we could as we drove along the highway. My uncle called with a travel update. I would be shuttled from the private airport to the commercial terminal to return to Boston with him. In those 15 minutes, with the help of Senator Kennedy, my father organized a consortium of doctors. Instead of sucking the triumph from the morning, that mood extended to envelop this complication. Nothing was beyond our abilities. We would fix this, too.

At the plane, the advisors stared at me, red-eyed and restless like huskies eager to take off in their race across the tundra. What had seemed so comfortable and familiar last night now seemed so different from my contemplative mood. I gave my father back to them and headed to the commercial terminal, where I sat with my uncle and stared out the windows.

The debates went on and I shuttled like an emissary between the two worlds, one of bedsides and hospital food, the other of secret locations and intensive debate preparation. On October 8 at Washington University in St. Louis, I sat in a folding chair outside the back door of the locker room, legs crossed, reading the paper as though I were waiting for a bus. In Arizona, I moved even farther away, outside the venue completely, shooting footage of the advisors, the protestors—who had multiplied into hangers-on—and college classmates of my father's whom I had never met. Keeping myself busy, I knew, was the best support I could give. Nobody wanted to watch me pace. I'm someone who gets nervous during sports games, when the stakes have only to do with the movement of a ball.

8

ELECTION

Overall voter turnout for the 2004 presidential election ended up being the highest since 1968, but Hawaii's pre-election poll numbers remained low among Democrats. Of the 50 states, it was ranked 50th—due in part to the large population of nonresident military, who cast absentee ballots in the states where they permanently resided. Despite these low numbers, the contest was so close that in the final days of the campaign I was sent there to campaign opposite Vice President Dick Cheney. I was met at the plane by Michael Paradise, an ironic name for the man who had been my trip advisor on most of my lone surrogate swings through various swaths of the country. When he placed a lei around my neck, I thought maybe I'd finally touched down in a spot that appropriately reflected his name. But then he plunged into a briefing, and the daydream I had of disappearing for a few days at a secluded lagoon disappeared. He steered me by my elbow and explained at a rapid-fire clip that we had an essential stop to make before I could be seen in public.

In Hawaii part of the cultural protocol—which I suspect is actually protocol only for visitors and tourists and possibly even an elaborate, extended practical joke Hawaiians good-naturedly play on the rest of us—is wearing a garment made of any fabric that Tom Selleck made popular during his tenure on *Magnum, P.I.* We walked through the mall looking for sarongs and dresses with the most toned-down collages of palm trees and pineapples. After discarding one Technicolor print after another, I begged again to wear the sundress I had packed, but Paradise shook his head implying that it was out of the question; by not appearing in "native dress," I would be insulting my hosts. I resigned myself to trying to find a minimally aggressive version.

At the rally that evening, I took the stage under the weight of eight brightly colored leis. I'd found the least offensive of the gaudy dresses, but the tradeoff was that it was three sizes too big. It flowed around me like a tropical tent. At least I was in good company. Vice President Al Gore was there also, making the best of a last-minute fashion fix; his embroidered white guayabera pulled slightly at the armholes. Though my father on occasion had reason to challenge my fashion decisions and I'd often resisted "dressing the part," in the last days of the campaign, I went in full costume as Annie Luau. At that stage I wouldn't have been surprised nor would I have protested, if Michael Paradise had greeted me at the next campaign stop in Portland with a stuffed giant mascot head and brown furry costume, explaining as he zipped me in that the people of Oregon preferred their campaigners dressed up as beavers.

Spending the last three days of October on a political vacation in Hawaii was surreal. I felt far away, not only from the contiguous United States, but also from the realities of the campaign. I stole away to the ocean to swim for a few minutes the next morning. In the water, conscious of my body's weight being lifted from me, I thought about the last image I had of my father. He had been standing against the brick wall of an auditorium in Ohio, waiting to go onstage at a campaign rally, relaxed and energized after playing a spontaneous backstage set with one of his favorite guitarists, Bruce Springsteen. I realized it was the last time I would see him before election night. The weightlessness I felt evolved into an emptiness that allowed waves of memories and emotions to pass through me. I was left with a bittersweet ache, a pronounced nostalgia, emotions like premonitions my practical mind hadn't had time to catch up with as the end of the journey grew closer. That night, I sat on the balcony of my hotel room with a friend who had come to join me on those last days of travel, drinking wine, talking about the events of the day, my mother, and what would happen next, and for some reason, in the middle of all that uncertainty, I felt a sense of peace. The damp tropical air grounded me. I looked at my bare feet that less than 48 hours earlier had been in heavy boots and allowed myself to laugh.

I don't remember arriving in Boston. Somewhere between Hawaii and the northeastern coast, I shed my sarong for a campaign staffer's overcoat that was a bit too small and put back on my shoes. I looked at my exposed wrists and pulled futilely at the sleeves—too short. I remembered nervously tugging at my cuffs when I'd been told in the fifth grade that my father was running for his first public office, lieutenant governor.

When he'd been elected that first time, we'd gathered as a family at home on Beacon Hill and walked the three blocks to the State House.

Now, on November 2, we were standing under the overhang of that same building, a few yards away from his first office as a public servant. The State House is a smaller replica of the US Senate building in Washington, DC, where he had occupied suites for the past 19 years. We were escorted through the corridors to the catacombs of the building, where we'd cast our votes. The press filled the basement hallways and the strange, empty room that had been cleared for our arrival. I was the last to enter the polling booth, which was stationed in the center of the room under a spotlight and looked like the kind of place where Clark Kent might change. Instead of moving slots or pulling levers, we were filling in paper ballots. It was hard to read which space to fill in. I studied the options, made sure I was lining up the right name with the corresponding circle, and finally pressed my pen into the paper. Drawing inside the circle felt like filling in a giant period on the entire year on the trail.

As I walked out of the basement and smiled for the press, I felt the familiar feeling of just having broken up with someone, wishing I could reduce the scattered moments to their truest meanings, take back the messy things I said, get it right one time before the end. The nostalgia was setting in before I was ready, before the relationship was even over.

The shock of the physical, definitive act of voting had forced me to finally confront the fact that my experience had really been about the product all along. We hadn't been campaigning in order to get to know a country; we had been campaigning to win. I don't remember how I traveled from one place to the next during the rest of that day. These final images play out in my memory like abstract scenes, an uncut movie, a play without transitions. The State House. A walk down the hill to get food. The hotel. In our rooms at the Copley Plaza, at the edge of a large common in downtown Boston, peripheral friends and financial supporters gathered in the lobby while close friends and random acquaintances took refuge in our suites. The day moved quickly. The morning sun turned into a dull rain by afternoon.

Conversations took on the feeling of a collage. Reporters called on phone lines that I had no idea they had the numbers to. The slowly mounting pressure of the forced intimacy of the campaign had finally broken through the fourth wall. Anonymous voices from a group I had struggled to maintain a distant relationship with were wishing me congratulations for a presidency that had yet to be won. "He's 15 points ahead," they said. "How do you feel?" These journalists, the omnipresent distant observers, were talking to me for the first time as friends, and while I took comfort in their assurances, I was skeptical; I knew polls and early returns didn't matter, yet I wanted to believe that it was over and that the journalists actually had the prescient knowledge they claimed to possess.

I watched the hands sweep across the face of my watch and studied the moving lines rearranging themselves on the digital clock by the bed. To distract myself, I turned to look at the crowds below the windows of the hotel room, the blurred faces that I realized had given me so much comfort throughout the past 12 months. I stared beyond them, at the temporary stage, red bunting hiding last-minute screws and bolts, and the American flag draped behind a podium, partially lit.

We were told we were going to leave for the stage at any minute, but the minute was continuously delayed, leaving us in a state of suspended animation. Beyond the walls of my hotel room, beyond the milling workers and supporters whom I saw filling the hallway every time the door opened, a distant sense of uneasiness built. I did my best to put it out of my mind. My attention felt both razor sharp and strangely foggy, jarred every 15 minutes by knocks at the door and someone apologizing, "Any minute now." I mentally rehearsed over and over again, like a looped film: the final knock on the door, shrugging on my coat, walking down the hall, riding in the service elevator, walking through the back corridors, through the hotel kitchen, and across the common. But we never walked our route. We never mounted the stage.

At midnight, the calls stopped. We were escorted from the hotel to our home on Beacon Hill, where my father and his advisors had set up camp. Through the giant glass panes of the windows in the hotel room I had seen the thousands of people waiting in front of the empty stage my father was supposed to take. For months I had been focused on the faces of strangers, and suddenly I was in our kitchen, watching the strained expressions of the campaign's advisors. I realized I had been so focused on the expressions of strangers that I had not studied the people I'd been most intimate with. Despite the shared pressures we all had felt, I had only really come to know a few personally. Now, in the kitchen, seeing their shocked and sorrowful faces that mirrored my own, finally allowed me to let go. Without speaking, we mourned together.

By virtue of the feeling in the house, I knew we had lost before anyone came out and declared it. I received calls from friends returning from Florida, trapped in vans with nothing but a radio echoing the returns from across the country, and from volunteers who had been working in Pennsylvania and arrived back in their apartments in New York to news that New Mexico had been lost. I can't remember how those late-night hours between the snippets of their voices passed. I don't know why I answered my phone each time a call came through. I suppose it was to connect to a world outside our bubble, which, though fragmented and weakening, was still the world I had known before all of this. A friend whispered in my ear, "The one person I am happy for is you because you get your life back."

I knew what she was trying to say, but I had never thought of my experience as a result of some sacrifice, at that moment least of all. It wasn't about my life or the lives of my family members; it was about the lives of those I'd had conversations with in Minnesota, Miami, and Colorado.

I felt the worst for the people who'd had the most to gain by voting, whose voices were silenced when their votes were suppressed. Later, we heard about a man, a union member and assembly-line worker turned plumber and a father of three. His parents grew up in the segregated South, marched in Selma, fought to eat at the lunch counter, suffered humiliations to attend school, and, though they could not afford to go to college, they made sure their grandchildren could.

He walked to the polling station in Cleveland filled with so much pride, believing his parents' sacrifices were not in vain.

He waited in line for hours. When his turn finally came, he was challenged at the polling station by a Republican lawyer, who told him that his identity could not be verified and his name had been stricken from the voter rolls. He noticed this happening to many others and objected vociferously. The person challenging his identity posited that maybe his name was too common, or maybe he was an ex-con. The volunteer jokingly suggested that the man, who had never in his life even tasted alcohol, was a drug dealer. He asked to speak to a supervisor, who told him that he could not vote, even though he had registered properly and had his identification with him. "But it's election day," he said. He was told he could wait in another line to file a complaint, which would mean he'd have to miss work. He asked himself what his parents would do, and he called in sick, choosing to vote, but his turn never came.

I'm not saying that the reason for our loss was solely the result of vote tampering or the actions of some insidious Republican machine. What saddened me was learning that the simplicity of the system set in place by the Constitution and modified to include blacks and women—"one citizen, one vote"—was in truth not a shining example of democracy, as my political science teacher had espoused during the moments when I had actually been listening. Like any system set up and run by individuals, it was vulnerable to manipulation and corruption.

The grandparents of the man whose vote was denied probably would have laughed at my naïveté. In spite of how hard we had campaigned, how diligently we had spread our message, asking only that people make the decision they saw fit to make, in the end, I realized that all of that still might not have been enough. Some of the most important parts of the process are beyond our control.

For many, the campaign was simply politics. But for me and many others, it was an adventure in humanity, will, faith, myth, and ritual. There was the photo op, and then there was the real moment after the reporters turned away. For all of the cynicism of politics, there was another side that was painfully human, brutally alive.

When I think about the moments of enthusiasm and frenzy, of the adrenaline that coursed through my body and animated me, I think of them as part of a quest I didn't even know I was on at the time. I found something I never even thought to seek, a strange and wild mixture of melancholy and pride. I learned that I care about this country, but not for the reasons I had thought.

At some point the importance of politics receded. Left in its wake were important questions about the fundamental direction of the nation, about war and peace, about our future. Watching the people who gathered backstage at rallies just to hand a bottle of water or a flag or a homemade sign to my father—it all began to make sense. Many of the people said they felt betrayed and confused by the corporate nature of politics and the politicians who climb the ladders of ambition like any other tradesman would. The people who gave up so much to join us on the trail understood that beyond the facade of political gamesmanship lay a deeper core: the steadfast desire to change the direction of the country. I couldn't bring myself to think about what this loss would cost them. I was told with official finality that we had lost on Wednesday morning, when my uncle David came into my room. His body was rigid, his shoulders were stiff with strain, as if he were carrying a heavy weight. "He's going to concede," he said. Still dressed in the clothes I had worn the night before, I reached for my scarf, fixing on the mundane task of tying it on. I willed myself to walk out into the icy morning.

To my family, Faneuil Hall was always more than just a historic building, a gathering place where many of the important moments in the American Revolution happened. It was a place where, when Vanessa and I were children, my father had entertained, educated, and sometimes bored us with historical details, as well as being a must-stop destination on myriad elementary school trips. But it was also where I'd sat in the audience listening to Ted Kennedy announce his candidacy for the 1980 presidential race; where, as a college student in 1996, I'd seen my father debate Bill Weld in a closely contested Senate race; and where my father had announced his own campaign for president—and now it was where that campaign would end.

My father revered Faneuil Hall not just for the reason the tour guides barked about—its role as the birthplace of American freedom during the days of the Boston Tea Party—but also for its place as a symbol of the American conscience, a place where abolitionists had dreamed of and demanded a nation that would live out its founding ideals of equality, from the fight for women's suffrage to the fight against fascism, from McCarthyism to civil rights. The walls of the place still reverberated with the rhetoric of honor, dissent, courage, and principle.

My father's words—"What we started in this campaign will not end here"—were stirring, but I wondered whether any of us there, cold and exhausted, could really hear him.

I did not know where to focus. As my father and then John Edwards spoke, I could digest little other than the rhythm of their words. I found myself staring at the podium and counting the scratches on the weathered wood. I forced myself to look at the eyes of the audience, to try to see what they were seeing and what, beyond them, the country was watching on television.

The pained look on the faces of the supporters made me uncomfortable, so I looked toward the press corps, hoping to find escape and comfort in the detached blankness of their stares. But my eyes landed on the face of a prominent writer for a news magazine, and beneath his glassy eyes, I saw the unmistakeable look of sadness and shame. And somehow, I shared it.

When people approach me to discuss their involvement in the campaign, it's seemed to me that the story is more theirs than mine—that although we shared the experience, people who had more distance from it might be better able to understand what it all meant. Sometimes, when I look back on it and try to share stories with friends, I am mired in a kind of quiet, an inability to express any feeling.

But in spite of having different micronarratives, one common impression prevails among those of us who shared the journey: When we lost, the energy was emptied from us with the same exacting impact as an earthquake. In some ways, it felt like a death.

I understood intellectually that after what had happened in 2000, it was a patriotic necessity for my father to quickly bring closure to the election, after having determined to his own satisfaction that Bush had won in Ohio, despite the massive voter suppression there and elsewhere. But still, I wanted to grieve and then move on, pretending, if possible, that the whole experience had never happened.

I have no solid memories of those first days after the election. In retrospect, I suppose I remember a wave of something salty and suffocating, an immense surge of energy that enveloped me and then was gone. I experienced a kind of disintegration. My feelings were disrupted images, chaotic drawings. Instead of forming a well-planned pattern that made sense of the experience, they were like haphazard lines falling outside the right angles of order, lines that looked like a moment of forfeit by a frustrated artist.

As loss is filtered through time, its meaning and dimensions change. I've tried to make sense of the experience since the election, but it's slippery: Some of the details have shifted or been misplaced. Trying to understand what we went through on the trail seems a bit like trying to understand something of too great a magnitude to easily digest, something too much for one person to carry. In the aftermath, I've often longed for an instruction manual, thinking to myself: There must be a simple blueprint, maybe an invisible map, that outlines the architecture and structures surrounding loss, tells us how to deal with the broken pieces that had held together the whole.

The end of the campaign merged in my mind with the diagnosis of the recurrence of my mother's cancer. Both of these events dissolved any fixed ideas I had had about loss and hope, about good luck and bad, and about destiny and our control over it. In the presence of something so monolithic and final, so essential and eternal, the structural artifacts become meaningless, the images I was able to capture with a camera showed me nothing other than additional pieces of an unsolvable puzzle.

After a two-year struggle with cancer, my mother, Julia Thorne, passed away on April 27, 2006.

I must admit that while it is comparatively easy to write about my father's losing the election, it is virtually impossible to write about my mother's passing. To write the obvious words that come to mind, like *pain* and *sadness*, is like trying to describe a complicated idea in a foreign language, a poor translation of experience. I am wary of expressing more of the specifics of how I felt, because it feels like a violation of her private memory. But to pretend that it didn't happen or to not mention it feels untrue.

In school, I remember studying other cultures that, unlike ours, accept loss as part of the life cycle of nature and train people to accept it. Americans are taught that they can conquer nature, conquer history, and conquer the consequences of their mistakes. We are taught that losing, and grieving over loss, are the results of weakness and failure, deserving pity at best and contempt at worst.

Our political system is not easy on the losers; its harshness doesn't encourage the people involved to share their true feelings and emotions. The strength that is applauded in candidates on the trail doesn't often reflect real, lived experience or true tests of character. Sometimes it seems as though the more stage-managed the persona is, the kinder the treatment the candidate gets from the public. And once you've seen what kind of dividends exposing yourself to the press yields, it's hard to ever feel totally free in a public sphere again. Everything can and will be used against you.

That certainly is true in politics, where noble losers are rare. Our winner-take-all system of presidential elections brutally imposes grief and loss; there are no coalition governments, no consolation prizes, no honorable positions of public trust for the losing candidates, however close the ballot result. And worse yet, there are no trophies to honor the passion and sacrifice of the hundreds of thousands of people who worked and prayed for a different outcome, or for the millions of voters who lost as well.

But many of these same people have their own stories of what this campaign meant to them, and each one owns the experience just as much as anyone else, including me. Many of them undoubtedly felt as numb as I did on that cold and unforgiving morning of November 3, 2004.

9

CONCLUSION

Four years ago I was preparing for a grueling summer of crisscrossing the nation in support of the Kerry-Edwards ticket, and if they had won, I would likely be preparing to do the same again—something, I must admit, I am happy I do not have to do. When I think of the process I participated in or watch as a bystander now, I choose not to focus on regret and anger. In part, I feel awed by the ability of politicians to withstand such relentlessly harsh treatment from the press and the nation, and in part I feel frustrated. It reminds me of a sentence I wrote in the margins of a book a long time ago that has always stuck with me: "We are far more primitive than we think we are."

Everything that is personal to a candidate becomes political, which only forces politicians deeper into their shells, hiding behind the images the media has created and the sound bites that seem to work best because they fear that if their real selves show through, something will be lost. It is not vanity; it is common sense and fear of the unknown. The risk, I suppose, is too great for candidates to let their guards down for even a split second and chance painfully human moments. And yet it was during my father's concession speech, when he was tired and emotional, that people said they related to him most.

Candidates' humanity ebbs as campaigns reach more televisions and radio programs and the process devolves into finger-pointing, spin, talking heads, and arduous efforts to stay ahead of the next news cycle. As citizens, we realize this about the process every four years, complain about it when it is done, and then repeat the game from scratch as if it had not been played with essentially the same rules for more than 200 years. The polity is broken up into so many polarized segments—white men with economic problems, well-educated soccer moms, Latina women who run small businesses, black men who never attend church—that we lose our unity as a nation and are told repeatedly about how divided we are that we actually begin to believe it. The press is forced to spend an election cycle recycling stories to fit into their audiences' expectations, pushing and prolonging a horse race. The press then spends a year commenting on its complicity with an unfair and undemocratic process, only to repeat the process four years later with no sense of irony.

Like Camus's insistence that we must imagine Sisyphus happy, I must imagine that while Don Delillo's barn has been photographed thousands of times, each picture that sits on someone's coffee table or mantel brings that person joy. Each picture, although it is essentially the same image, is unique because each person captured one fleeting moment that became a part of the fabric of his or her personal story.

I participated in one of the most watched, photographed, filmed, blogged about, and studied events of the last decade, and until now the most photographed presidential election in history. Even as we all look at the same pictures, we each have our own stories to tell about them.

I will never forget seeing America through a dusty bus window as it hurtled at 80 miles per hour through the desert. I will never forget the bite of the Iowa cold or the smell of the ocean air in Hawaii in the minutes before a campaign event began. I will never forget the tension that resulted when small, minor family outings turned into photo ops. I can close my eyes and drift over the receiving lines—once teeming with life and noise, now quiet in the dead of winter—or the sites of my father's major addresses on foreign policy or health care. I can feel the moments captured in these images as if I were just there. They each feel as sharp as the one of me sitting against the plastic of my elementary school chair, staring out the window at the the sky, and wondering what it would be like to be older. In those brief minutes between campaign events, in those ephemeral afternoons when everything seemed possible and nothing seemed wrong, when summer prolonged the days and I watched the sun over western lakes and Florida byroads, it did not seem to matter who won or lost.

10

IMAGES

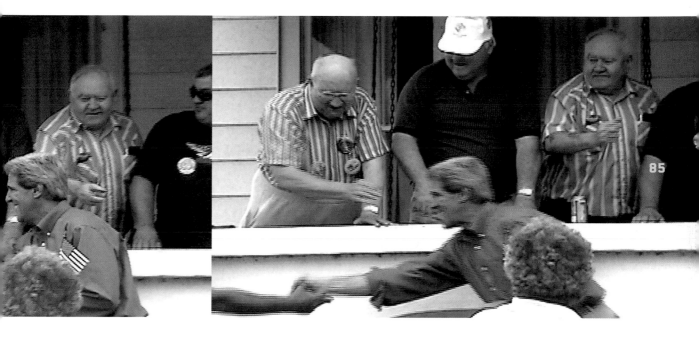

92

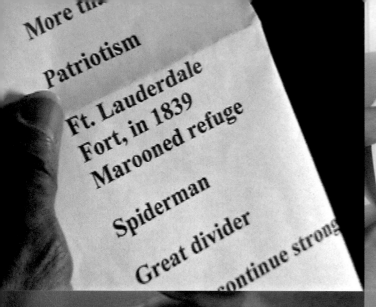
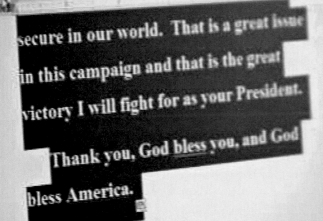

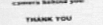
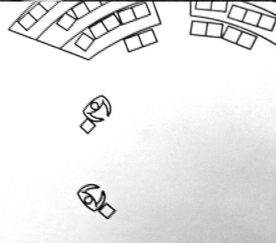

105

109

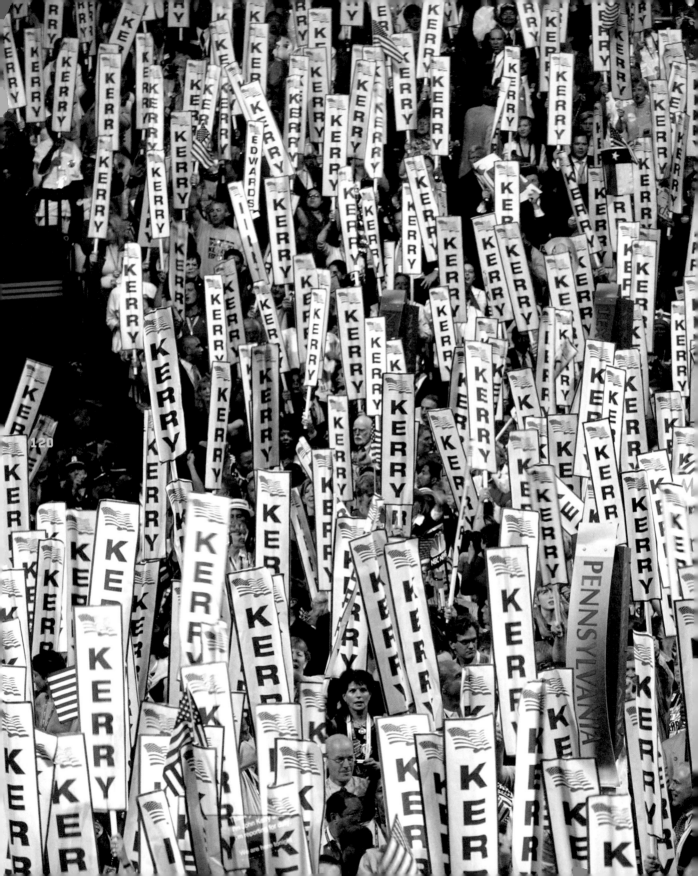

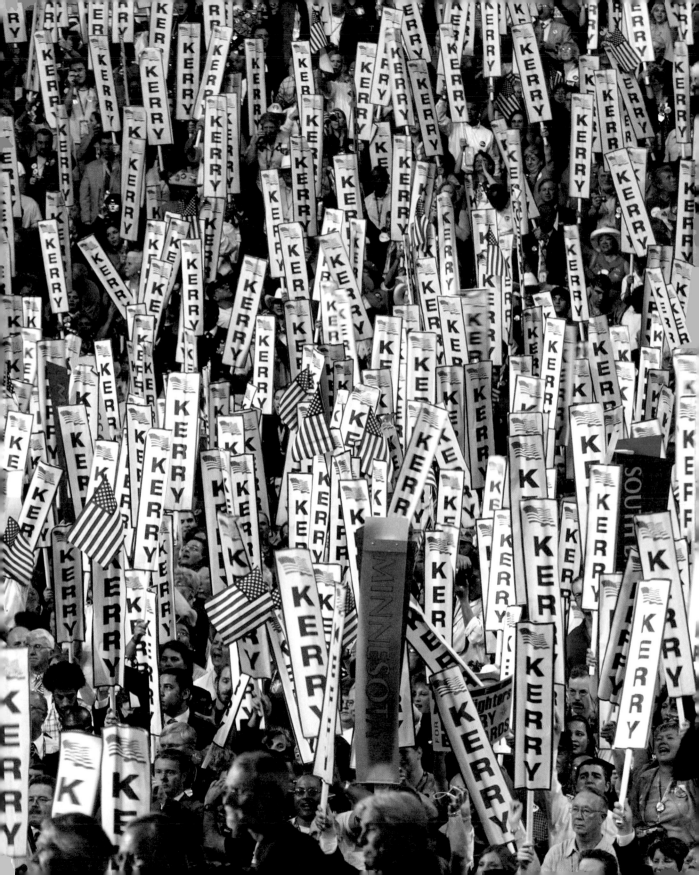

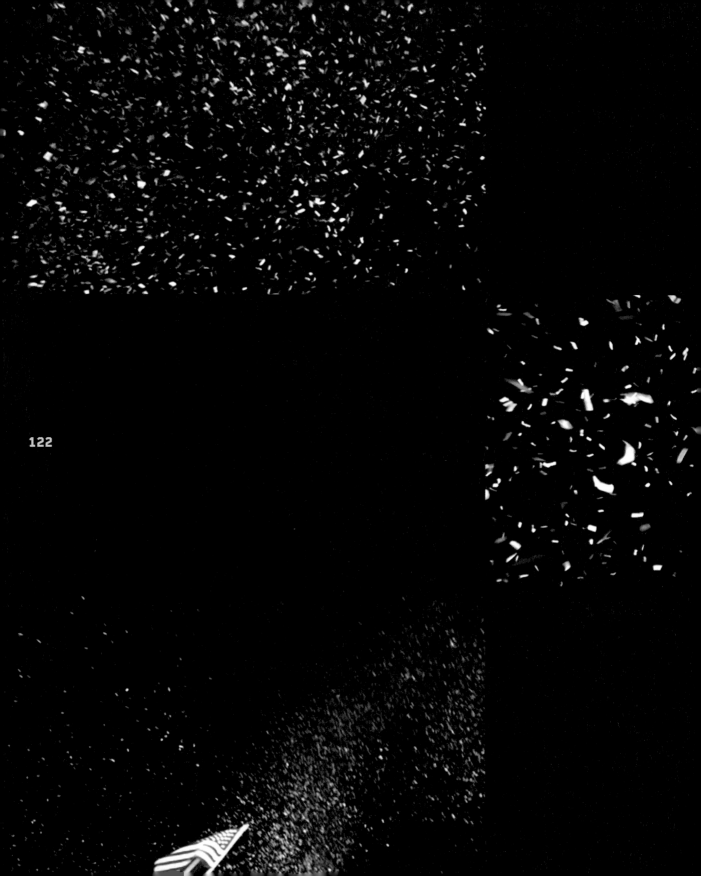

122

124

www.swillvets.com

132

134

138

152

162

165

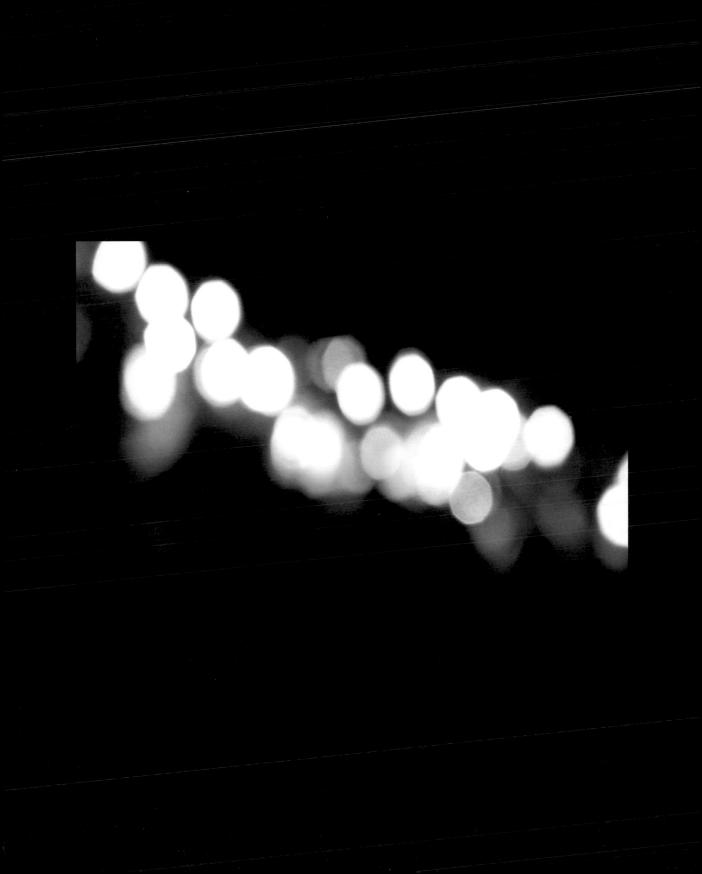

EPILOGUE

In 2004, 10 million more votes were cast for the Democratic candidate than in 1996 and 5 million more than in 2000. In 2008, the Democratic Party has kept that enthusiasm alive, building upon it daily. As I write, the race for the Democratic presidential nomination between Barack Obama and Hillary Clinton may have had its divisive moments, but among the party's rank and file, it generates interest and passion of an intensity that is significantly greater, by several measures, than that in the uncontested Republican contest.

It is nothing short of breathtaking that only a few generations after African Americans and women were granted the right to vote, the two front-runners for the Democratic nomination were a black man and a woman. This historic moment certainly has contributed to the unprecedented degree of engagement of members of the Democratic party with the nomination process.

A 2007 Pew Research Center survey found that 57 percent of Democrats said the Democratic campaign was "very interesting" whereas only 32 percent of young Republicans found their party's contest engaging. No doubt enthusiasm among Democrats will increase as the general election campaign begins in earnest.

In many ways, some aspects of the conversation in 2008 were predicated by the contest in 2004. To take just one example, the "swiftboating" of candidates—and how best to avoid it—has entered the political lexicon.

Beyond what the pundits said, what the clips replayed on CNN for years to come will imply, and what the consultants' endless analysis will conclude, my experience changed me from someone who was uninterested in politics, who thought it was all a game, who did not trust the process, who feared that the system was broken, into someone who feels that although the system remains problematic, it is also vital—a powerful feeling considering that the outcome was not one I favored. It took time for me to move beyond the experience, to slow myself down and process the campaign, to figure out what it meant, but in the end I am left with a comforting sensation that the process is complicated but alive and dynamic.

In April 2008, I stood on a street corner in New York City in the rainy predawn hours. As I waited for the Obama campaign carpool to pick me up at the designated location, I watched the stragglers weave home from last calls at local bars and listened to a disheveled couple start up a familiar fight as they climbed out of a taxi, the man sighing, "Here we go again."

Of course, it would be different for me this time, as one of the foot soldiers piled into the Toyota minivan to do door-to-door canvassing in the weeks leading up to the Pennsylvania primary as opposed to one of the surrogates whisked from one predesignated location to another in a carefully orchestrated pattern.

This time instead of Michael Paradise there was only the disembodied voice of the GPS system, whom we dubbed "Debbie." Debbie seemed to have a weak grasp of directions but spoke in an assured voice that lulled us all into a false sense of security until we realized how lost we were somewhere near the New Jersey/Pennsylvania border. I sat in the back of the van with other volunteers, including a few friends, listening to our driver and the campaign coordinator bicker about the location of our destination, Stoneyfork, while from the dashboard Debbie played unknowing moderator in a haunting monotone.

By the time we arrived, the rally had begun. It was smaller than I had expected, a half-full school auditorium. It struck me that most of the meetings or gatherings I had attended previously had been events where the candidate himself was scheduled to appear—the headlining rallies, the big draws. There were smaller gatherings like this happening all the time that I had never seen, gatherings of enthusiastic volunteers who made the campaign happen. My perspective had been blurred by the curtain of confetti that it seemed was always falling then, separating me from those seas of faces I was now solidly among.

The rally might have been smaller, but the energy and enthusiasm was inspiring. I watched from the audience as Caroline Kennedy and Jessica Lange spoke of their connection to the candidate, rousing the group of people who had driven from as far as Florida for the day of canvassing. Women in red shirts swarmed the stage; they had come from Massachusetts and assumed the postures and poses of a cheerleading squad on the stage for a photo op.

The organization that went into a national campaign revealed itself as we were handed our packets of maps, driving directions, flyers, informational talking points and scripts, should we be at a loss for what to say. There were also rating scales attached to our paper that taught us how to identify a home's interest. If the principal concern was the environment, it would be marked with a "3." If the homeowners desired more information on education, it would be given a "4." If they were Latino, it got a "1." If they were Latinos who cared equally about the environment and education, we decided we would just make something up.

We drove past the traditional stone houses of Bucks County, mini-malls, and row after row of suburban homes. I hadn't been outside of New York in about two months and the clean air and orderly spaces between buildings made me feel alien in my urban black attire. I had discarded the reluctantly learned lessons of political dressing with great relief at the end of the last campaign, but as we passed one split level after another, I remembered the practical reasons for dressing in as nonthreatening and universally appealing way as possible and wondered if it would be harder to convey the message.

We pulled over where the campaign's Google map printout indicated, on the side of an empty street banked by chemical green lawns, and made our way toward the faux stone entrance sign of "Riverside Estates." We broke into groups of two or three, held up our maps, and followed the red dots on the map that pointed out the houses where registered Democrats lived. As we walked the perfect blacktop, its inky surface unmarred by any tire tracks, and the pink cherry blossoms marked the first flush of spring overhead, I rehearsed my political speak. I hoped I would remember what to say, how to comfortably discuss issues, how to connect with people we met for the first time. I thought about the best way to explain why we had volunteered. I figured when the time came, it would all come back to me.

My preparation was unnecessary. At the first ten houses no one answered the door. I couldn't tell if they were hiding from us, thinking we were some kind of urban Jehovah's Witnesses, or whether they honestly weren't at home. It was impossible to tell from the number of cars in the driveway. Each house seemed to have three or four cars at a minimum, and from what I could tell, the number didn't correlate in any way to the number of people in the house. After the eleventh doorbell went unanswered, in the back of my head I heard Debbie from the GPS system suggest we turn back or lie down in the grass for a rest.

Lost in the tangle of roads lined with houses that suggested similarity, we followed the red dots on our map as though they were bread crumbs. I heard a baby crying from behind a closed door and girded myself for a potential discussion. A white, middle-aged single father answered the door. Faced with a real live voter for the first time in four years, I forgot everything. Luckily we had the script: "Hello my name is (insert name). I am here on behalf of the Obama campaign, and I was wondering if you have decided who you will vote for on primary day."

He stuttered with his answers but had insights about the race. Early that morning, CNN and ABC began their round-the-clock news coverage of Reverend Jeremiah Wright's diatribe. Even though the man believed in a lot of what Obama stood for, as a Jewish American, he was turned off by the reverend's affect and the content of his speech. The man didn't see how he could possibly vote for Obama with a clear conscience. Nothing about this in the script. We managed smiles and asked him to take a flyer before he closed the door.

After three hours walking the same-seeming streets, getting little or no response, we turned down a cul-de-sac where the only person in sight was a little boy dribbling a basketball in the driveway of his house. As we approached, we saw an elderly woman who stared at us from her guardian position near the front porch. The boy grabbed the ball out of the air, tucked it under his arm, and approached us.

"Are you the police?" he asked. An interesting guess considering our appearance.

"No," I said. "We're here from the Obama campaign." I was determined to stay on message, no matter the audience.

"Oh cool," he said while dribbling his ball in long, drawn-out rhythms. Then he looked up at me through the overgrown fringe of his bangs, squinted, and asked, "Hey, are you John Kerry's daughter?"

"Sometimes," I answered, an inadvertent tic I quickly corrected. "No, no, yes."

"Oh cool," he said, with as much excitement as he might have had if I'd told him that I could shoot death-ray beams out of my eyes. After a pause the boy explained, "I voted for him in 2004."

"You did?" I said, going along with it. After all, this was the most engaged citizen I had talked to all day, even if he wasn't older than ten or eleven.

"Yeah, I voted for him all right." After confirming this, he changed direction. "Are you famous?" He demanded. I didn't answer this question, which seemed like an obvious trap.

"No, but . . . who are you voting for this time?" I asked.

"I can't decide," he frowned. "I watch the news and I think I'm going to vote for Obama but . . . I can't decide."

"Well, what do you think about when you're trying to make your decision?" He stopped dribbling and started balancing the ball on his middle finger, silent in concentration until it fell and rolled away.

"I don't know. You know, I really like the Democratic platform. But you know we've worked really hard for our money here in the suburbs and as much as we want to help the poor, it's very difficult when we have to give half of our earnings to taxes." He pushed his glasses up on his nose and waited for a reply.

"By any chance, is your dad a Republican?" I glanced up at the woman I presumed was his grandmother, and she took off her sunglasses, revealing deep set eyes accented with fluorescent violet eye shadow. She stepped toward us and said, "Yes, his dad is. But his mother and I are Democrats. The boy's got both influences. It makes him a little confused from time to time."

"I see," I said, turning toward her. "And who are you going to vote for?"

"My daughter and I have been talking about it. We just don't know," she said.

We talked with her as she had stepped forward, let go of her glasses, and started asking questions. When we left, she was unconfirmed either way, but she promised to think about it. She thanked us for the information. As I turned down the L-shaped walkway, her grandson called out, "I decided."

ACKNOWLEDGMENTS

Countless people collaborated and assisted in the making of this book.

Thank you to the people on the campaign, the advisors, and secret service who tolerated my camera in 2004, especially John Sasso, Setti Warren, Marvin Nicholson, Stephanie Cutter, David Morehouse, Wendy Grey, and Jim Loftus.

And thanks to the many pens and personalities who made up the press corps.

I would also like to thank the people who helped in the filming process: To Rosadel Valera and Gabby Adler who helped organize production and schedules from the ground. And to Rocket Science Labroratory and Viks Patel who helped quiet the images and assisted in transforming the film into a book.

I would also like to recognize the commitment, curiosity, humor, and eye of my other shooters on the documentary—Mona Eldaif, Sherief Elkatsha, Paul Boyzymowski, Roo Rogers, Jehane Noujaim, and Tanaz Eshaghian—who helped frame so many moments as I snuck them on planes and subjected them to hours of security searches in post 9/11 public airports.

Thanks to the photographers whose images accompany mine and who worked with me on the visual narrative: Dina Rudick, Hector Mata, and C. J. Gunther.

Thanks to Ed Kilgore and Elyse Lightman, and especially Nicholas Arons and David Wade, who assisted in the construction of the book in its earliest stages.

Thanks to Leigh Haber who shepherded the book into Rodale and to Shannon Welch who shepherded it out.

A special thank you to Shannon for staying in the trenches with me and helping me bring the project to life. She gave me necessary outside perspective while offering a new lens to look through. Without her, this book would not exist.

This book would also not exist without the patience, creativity, and help of Erica Beeney, who structured the manuscript, lent ideas and words, and with patience and persistence, encouraged me to put one sentence together at a time.

Thanks to Andy Carpenter for supporting an independent streak and to designers David Heasty and Stefanie Weigler for interpreting my vision and integrating their own interpretation and knowledge.

Special thanks to Mel Berger, William Morris, Jeremy Barber, Jason Burns, the United Talent Agency, and Todd Rubenstein.

To Scott Carneal who told me to write if all else failed.

Thank you to early readers and editors, both friends and family: Zoe Wolff, John Mailer, Matt Pascarella, Vanessa Kerry, Eloise Lawrence, David Thorne, Leonie Kruizenga, and Evan Schindler.

To "jk" for believing in something larger than himself and teaching me about a national generosity. And to Julia Thorne, who was always waiting on a land line and who is not able to see the finished product of the journey. I dedicate this book to her.